GCSE RELIGIOUS STUDIES for AQA

TRUTH, SPIRITUALITY AND CONTEMPORARY ISSUES

Richard Beck
David Worden

Heinemann Educational Publishers
Halley Court, Jordan Hill, Oxford, OX2 8EJ
a division of Reed Educational & Professional
Publishing Ltd

OXFORD MELBOURNE AUCKLAND
JOHANNESBURG BLANTYRE GABORONE
IBADAN PORTSMOUTH NH(USA) CHICAGO

Text © Richard Beck, David Worden, 2001
First published in 2002

05 04 03 02
9 8 7 6 5 4 3 2 1

British Library Cataloguing in Publication Data
A catalogue record for this book is available from the
British Library

ISBN 0 435 306928

Picture research by Jennifer Johnson
Typeset by Artistix, Thame, Oxon
Printed and bound in Italy by Printer Trento S.R.L

Acknowledgements
The authors would like to thank the following for the
use of copyright material: AQA on pp. 33, 49, 65, 81,
97; Reproduced with permission of mediawatch-uk on
p. 71; United Christian Broadcaster on p. 75; The
Voluntary Euthanasia Society on p. 40.

The authors and publishers would like to thank the
following for the use of copyright material:
Associated Press/Chuck Robinson on p. 91; The
Bridgeman Art Library/British Library, London on p. 6;
Camerapress/Gavin Smith on p. 70; Camerapress/
Richard Stonehouse on p. 67; Camera Press London/
Peter Abbey on p. 91; Circa Photo Library/John Smith
on p. 107; Corbis/Reuters New Media Inc. on p. 36;
Corbis/Roger Ressmeyer on p. 45; Empics/Steve
Mitchell on p. 98; Empics/Neal Simpson on p. 50;
Format/Ulrike Preuss on p. 34; Sally and Richard
Greenhill/Richard Greenhill on p. 43; Sally and Richard
Greenhill/Sally Greenhill on p. 20; Hutchison Picture
Library/Crispin Hughes on p. 108; The Kobal
Collection on p. 23; The Kobal Collection/D.C. Comics
Inc. on p. 23; Macmillan Cancer Relief on p. 35;
Christine Osborne Pictures on pp. 8, 47 and 100; Panos
Pictures/Sean Sprague on p. 38; Photofusion/Crispin
Hughes on p. 102; Rex on p. 86; Rex/Alban Donahoe
on p. 82; Rex/Tony Kyriacou on p. 4; Samaritans on
p. 37; Science Photo Library on p. 2; Science Photo
Library/Kevin Beebe/Custom Medical Stock Photo
on p. 24; Science Photo Library/Petit Format/Nestle
on p. 18.

The publishers have made every effort to trace the
copyright holders, but if they have inadvertently
overlooked any, they will be pleased to make the
necessary arrangements at the first opportunity.

Cover photograph by Photodisc

Tel: 01865 888058   www.heinemann.co.uk

Section 1 Nature and expression 2

Section 2 Religious responses to contemporary issues 18

Matters of life 18

Matters of death 34

Drug abuse 50

Media and technology 66

Crime and punishment........................... 82

Rich and poor in society 98

Glossary 115

Index 119

Aim
To understand the nature of truth.

What is truth?

Many people see religion as a search for truth. By exploring religious ideas, they hope to find answers to the mysteries of life. Some people and some religions claim that they have the truth. They believe that the lives and teachings of religious leaders, the sacred writings of their religion and their own personal experience provide the answers to what life is all about. They know what to believe, how they should live their lives and what they must do to gain eternal life or release from a cycle of rebirths.

But what is truth? At first, the answer to this question might seem very simple. The truth is correct – it is right; it is not false or wrong. Telling the truth means being honest and not telling lies. Something is true if we can prove it. A true story actually happened; it is fact, not fiction.

By giving these sorts of answers we often open up other questions. How do we know and how can we be certain that something is true? How can we prove that something is true and what sort of proof would convince us? The answers to these questions may vary according to the type of truth we are talking about.

Scientific truth

The sun rises in the east and sets in the west. We know this to be true because we see it happen every day. By **observation**, we can establish this to be a truth about the world we live in. However, observation alone can mislead us. The language we use to describe this daily event suggests the sun is the object that moves. This was believed for many centuries. We now know that the earth moves around the sun. In the 3rd century BCE, the idea was put forward that the earth revolves on its own axis. In scientific terms, this is called a **hypothesis**. But it was not until the nineteenth century that Jean Foucault (1819–68) carried out his famous **experiment** using the pendulum to mark the movement of the earth.

Foucault used scientific methods to prove the movement of the earth

This provided proof based on evidence. Although science may seem to be full of facts, proofs and certainties, it is always changing. New evidence and more experiments can often lead scientists to change their minds.

Historical truth

King Henry VIII had six wives. We know this from people who wrote at the time and the documents that record his reign. Later historians have also confirmed this by their research. There is enough evidence to give us the proof we need to say this statement is true. We can be satisfied that the statement is historically true. Historical evidence is often used in answering questions about the origins of religions and the lives of founders. It can establish facts about the past and can also be used to make judgements about the past. It is true to say that Henry VIII had six wives; it is a matter of judgement to say he misused his power. Judgements rely upon evidence, but are affected by people's opinions. These may be supported by reasons but are still a matter of interpretation. It is possible to have plenty of evidence, but no proof and to draw different conclusions from the same evidence.

Moral truth

Murder is wrong. Is that true? Most people, almost without thinking, would say yes. If we were to ask how they know it is true, they might say, 'It just is,' or 'My conscience tells me it is'. Unlike scientific truth, there is no experiment to prove moral truth. In other words, this is a different form of truth. It often depends upon **abstract reasoning** to reach a conclusion. For example, would the people who believe murder to be wrong say that it is true at all times and in all circumstances? If so, we can call it a **moral absolute**, because there are no exceptions to the rule. However, would it be wrong to murder a gunman about to shoot women or children? What about euthanasia, can that ever be right? What begins as a simple statement, which you probably thought was true, is perhaps much more complicated. You may have decided that the truth is now not absolute but **relative**; that circumstances can change the truth.

Spiritual truth

'My soul will live on after I am dead.' Is this true? This form of truth is a matter of belief. It is also personal. The statement might be true for the person who makes it, but it may not be true for other people. Not everyone believes we have a soul; not everyone believes in life after death. Life after death is a probability not a certainty. Beliefs of this sort may come from reading sacred writings, studying the teachings of founders or listening to the words of religious leaders. They may then rely upon **reason** to arrive at the truth. However, most people would say that religion is not about logical arguments. Faith may also come from a religious experience. People who have a strong faith may believe that God has spoken to them or revealed himself in some way. Those who have faith may count these sorts of **experience** as evidence for the truth of their beliefs and provide them with certainty, but they are not proof. They take us into the world of spirituality.

❓ Questions

1 How do scientists try to establish the truth?
2 How do historians try to establish the truth?
3 What is moral truth about?
4 What sorts of experiences might people have to support their faith?
5 What is the difference between evidence and proof?

📖 For discussion

1 'For something to be true you must be able to prove it.' How far do you agree? C2.1a
2 Take a simple moral statement, which at first sight appears to be absolutely true, for example, 'It is wrong to steal' or 'It is wrong to tell lies'. Can you think of any situations when it would be right to break such a rule? C2.1a

◆ For research

Find out how Foucault used scientific method to prove the Earth rotates. Go to the Internet website: www.calacademy.org. Enter 'Foucault' in the search box then select 'About Foucault Pendulums'. It is an animated site. IT1.1

Aim
To understand the nature of spirituality.

Consumer society

We are all consumers. We live in a **consumer society**. Our bodies consume food, our cars consume fuel and our homes consume energy. In all cases, often far more than necessary. We know that most of this consumption is not good for either us or our environment. Many people try to cut down on their consumption for a variety of reasons. They try to eat less, often because they want to lose weight; they buy smaller cars to save on petrol and introduce energy saving devices in their homes to reduce their bills. All these things also help to preserve the environment and save money. Money, however, is something that there tends to be plenty of when it comes to shopping. Clothes, for example, are not just items to cover our bodies.

Shopping plays an important part in a consumer society

Designers and advertisers want us to believe that we are what we wear, that our clothes say something about us as individuals. To make an impression, you need this season's fashions, in the right colours with a designer label, and you need to carry the latest mobile phone. This shows that you can look good, have both money and style, and are a successful member of the consumer society. You have signed up to **materialism**. Inside the clothes, there is a voice that says, 'If I have the most and best of everything, I'll feel better and be happier.' The problem is that the feeling will probably wear off faster than the clothes wear out and that 'keeping up with the Jones's' is a never ending and expensive battle.

The spiritual dimension

Some people take a different view of life. They believe that whatever we wear on the outside will never permanently change what is on the inside. No matter how many material things we own, they will not touch us spiritually.

The spiritual side of life is not bound by the physical world, it extends to a different dimension. It gives meaning and purpose to existence and a way of interpreting and understanding what happens to us. It values the world and other people, but puts both in the context of a greater existence. It extends beyond this life into the possibility of a life after death.

Spiritual experience

Experience of this spiritual dimension can come in a variety of ways. The difficulty is in trying to put the experience into words. Attempts to say what it is will always fall short of a satisfactory explanation. In *One moment*, Leggo, a 16-year-old from Australia, describes the experience of love as, '*The most amazing moment in my entire life, when everything suddenly seemed so much clearer.*'

One moment

It was like I was flying and drowning at the same time, it was insane, it was chaotic, it was … so surreal and so incredibly and beautifully overwhelming. The moment when my whole view changed, the way I saw the world, how I remembered people, how I perceived events, it changed. And I became a better person for it. I was spiralling, dizzyingly changing and merging into humanity, which is cruel and kind, and it was magnificent and awe-inspiring and it hurt. It hurt like crazy. I was burning, melting, freezing into what I had become. I had become a victim to my passions, not a ruler of them, and that is when the truth became obvious. No matter how twisted and shattered my life may be, all I want is for others to experience what I have felt. To become victims of their passions, to melt into humanity and to completely and entirely sacrifice themselves to others. I want them to love, to be loved, and that they must realize that love doesn't just happen, like Hollywood has scripted, we enable it to happen by acting upon the actions that actualize it, vulnerability and wounding are the keys to love and opening these wounds is the feeling of life, of freedom, of acceptance. There is no such philosophy as the meaning of life, it's the feeling of life … and that is what the lonely people seek.

These words express more than just emotion. They struggle to relate a profound moment in time. They show that some experiences can give us a whole new feeling about our relationships, the world and ourselves, about who we are and how important we are.

Moments of spiritual experience can come at any time and when least expected, as in the next passage.

Monday, 24 May 1875

This afternoon I walked over to Lanhil. As I came down from the hill into the valley across the golden meadows and among the flower-scented hedges, a great wave of emotion and happiness stirred and rose within me. I know not why I was so happy, nor what I was expecting, but I was in a delirium of joy; it was one of the supreme few moments of existence, a deep delicious draught from the strong sweet cup of life. It came silently, suddenly, and it went as it came, but it left a lingering glow and glory behind as it faded slowly like a gorgeous sunset, and I shall ever remember the place and the time in which such great happiness fell upon me.

Francis Kilvert's Diary, Francis Kilvert

Spiritual experiences are often associated with times of being alone and close to nature. The sight of a spectacular sunset, a snow-capped mountain or a river can fill people with a sense of awe, wonder and mystery.

The arts can also provide similar experiences. These work in two ways. Composers, painters, architects, choreographers and poets, for example, may feel that what they are producing comes not just from themselves, but from a greater source of inspiration. When we see or listen to their work, we may experience tingling sensations or be moved to great joy or sadness. Everyone can have such experiences, but they may not call them religious. That is a matter of interpretation. People who do not have a faith may see them as part of the mystery of life, the wonder of nature or the greatness of human achievement. For those who already have a faith, they support their belief and bring them closer to the Divine.

? Questions

1 What do we mean by 'a consumer society' and 'materialism'?
2 Why are some people so interested in consumer goods?
3 What view might a religious person take of consumerism?
4 What words do Leggo and Francis Kilvert use to describe their experiences?

For discussion

1 'The richer we are, the happier we are.' How far do you agree? C2.1a
2 What is your view of life?

For research

1 Find out about 'near death' experiences. How far do they support a spiritual view of life? C1.2
2 Find out about someone who has had a religious experience in one of the faiths you are studying. C1.2

Aim

To understand:

- religious claims to truth made by sacred writings and religious authorities
- conscience as a source of truth.

If you have faith in someone, or you put trust in a friend, you believe the person will not let you down. Most religious people, with the exception of Buddhists, believe in God. They put their faith and trust in Him and in the religion that helps them to understand and become closer to Him.

Belief and truth

If you belong to a religion, you are likely to say that your religion is true. It must be true for you, otherwise you would not believe in it. As you believe your religion to be true, you would probably go on to say that it possesses the truth. At this point, disagreements can start to occur. There would be no problem if only one religion existed in the world or if we accepted the idea that two opposing views can both be right. There are, however, many religions and most people believe that only one view can be right. This means that religions often make conflicting claims to the truth. Buddhism says there is no God. Other religions believe that God exists.

An outside observer might say that each religion has something to say about the truth and none of them has all the truth. Of course, not all religions would agree with this.

Sacred writings

Each of the six major religions of the world has sacred writings. They are also known as holy books and scriptures. Within a religion, there may be several important writings. Often, there is one that is more important than all the others and is regarded as *the* holy book. This has a higher status or position than the others and is usually treated with great respect.

Authority and inspiration of sacred writings

Sacred writings have authority within their religions. This means that people can refer to them to find teachings that provide the basic beliefs of the faith. They may also contain a life of the founder, a history of the religion, stories, instructions for worship and rules of behaviour. It often depends on how they came to be written as to how much authority they have.

Muslims, for example, believe that God revealed the Qur'an to Muhammad, who recited it word for word to others, who later wrote it down.

As it came directly from God, it is the absolute authority in Islam. By contrast, the teachings in the Buddhist scriptures were passed down from one generation to another for several centuries before being written down.

Some Christians have a similar view to Muslims. They believe the Bible is the word of God and is free from any mistakes. Another view involves the idea of inspiration. This can take two forms. One is that the writers believed God was active in the world and they were inspired to put their understanding of Him into writing.

The importance of scriptures is often shown by their lavish decoration

The other form is that God passed His message on to selected people who wrote it down as they understood it.

Interpretation of sacred writing

You do not read a book of science fiction in the same way as you would read a science textbook. You would also know the difference between a history book and a work of historical fiction. In English, you will have learned about similes and metaphors and you will understand the difference. You may know some parables and you might have heard of an allegory. These are all different types of writing. To understand them properly, we need to know what they are like and how they work. This is called their nature. A parable is a story that may or may not be based on actual events and the point of the story is in its meaning. That is the nature of a parable. It is not in its nature to be historical or scientific. Scriptures contain many different types of writing. You need to know which type you are dealing with in order to interpret it properly.

Not all religious people necessarily agree on the nature of a piece of writing. For example, some believe writings about the creation of the world to be literally true, that what is written is what happened. Others believe that they are stories that illustrate the belief that God is the creator of the world. How people interpret sacred writings also depends on what they believe about their authorship and inspiration. This in turn affects the claims to truth that can be made for them.

Religious authorities

There are also other types of religious authority. Some people attach importance to traditions because they reflect the way the religion has developed over the years and how God has led His people to a deeper understanding of their faith. People find truth in traditions because they have stood the test of time.

Leaders play an important part in all religions and are often a source of authority in interpreting the faith. In Christianity, the pope is the head of the Roman Catholic Church. He can speak with authority on behalf of the church because people believe he is elected by bishops, but chosen by God.

Within religions, there are also institutions, such as the Sangha in Buddhism and the Khalsa in Sikhism. Institutions are usually made up of groups of people. They have authority because they are either elected or initiated after a period of training and are therefore respected.

Conscience

These forms of authority can play an important part in making decisions about what is right and wrong. Some people, however, will also trust their own judgement. They believe they are guided from within themselves by their **conscience**. Your conscience can be thought of as the person you have silent conversations with when you are deciding how to behave. It will often tell you to do the right thing when you want to do the wrong thing.

But what is it? Religious people may say it is the Voice of God telling them what to do. Non-religious people may describe it as an agent of inner truth, something we are born with. Some people see the conscience as something we learn, it grows as we develop in our surroundings and is therefore a product of social environment.

? Questions

1 What sort of qualities would you expect the person you trust to have?
2 How can you interpret the story of the blind men and the elephant?
3 What do religious people mean when they say sacred writings are inspired?
4 Explain the difference between traditions, leaders and institutions.

For discussion

1 'Sacred writings are the most important form of authority.' How far do you agree? C2.1a
2 'Your conscience is the best guide in life.' How far do you agree? C2.1a

For research

Find out what sort of authority a local religious leader has in your community.

Being a religious person is not just about having a set of beliefs; it is a way of life. People who have a particular faith see the world differently from other people. Their behaviour and the attitudes they have are an expression of their beliefs. Religious people like to share their faith with others who have the same beliefs. This leads them to meet with other members of their religion or even live together in religious communities.

Expression of individual commitment

We all have a need to express our feelings. We know what it means to experience happiness or disappointment and these emotions can be seen in how we look and behave. How we look and behave is not the emotion itself, but an outward expression of it. The emotion is actually within us. People who believe in God often want to express their love for Him and to grow closer to Him. One way religious people do this is through worship.

The first time you see or take part in an act of worship, you may feel like you are entering a different world. In many ways you are. Worship is an attempt to show the worth, value and importance of God, to honour Him and become closer to Him and to show your goal in the next life. Worship is the outward expression of an inner spiritual world. Some people say they can be closest to God when they are still and quiet; when there is nothing around to distract them or to interrupt their concentration. For this reason some religious buildings may seem very bare.

Some types of worship involve people using different forms of **physical movement** or adopting certain positions. **Yoga** is an example of this, so is kneeling or holding your hands together. Many people feel they need the **physical discipline** of controlling the body before they can control the mind. These physical acts then combine with the mental aspects of **prayer** and **meditation**.

In its extreme form, this is known as **mysticism** and may involve the person in leading a life of contemplation away from the rest of society, often alone.

Very few religious people are mystics, however. Most prefer a form of **piety**, or religious devotion, that involves being with others. Many of these also like to have things to help them in their worship. A simple **artefact**, like a rosary, is used in several religions as an aid to worship. Special clothes worn by religious leaders during worship, statues and **ritual objects** used in ceremonies also have symbolic meanings. A **symbol** reminds people of important parts of their faith and provides a focus for worship.

Spiritual expression is not just confined to worship. Religious creativity exists in art, literature, music, architecture, dance and drama. In all these areas people use their skills to express their faith and help the spiritual development of others.

Some forms of worship involve meditation

Membership of a faith community

Some people believe they have a spiritual calling to lead a special life with other members of their faith. If so, they may join a **religious community** and share a communal lifestyle. Many of these communities are **monastic**. Here, people take vows and decide to spend the whole of their lives as members of a religious order. This tradition is found in Christianity and Buddhism. Hinduism also has various forms of religious communities. Other people may join a community for a shorter period, anything from a weekend to a few years, or on a regular basis, perhaps one weekend a month. Such a visit is often called a **retreat**, because it gives people the chance to retreat, or step away, from the normal routines of their lives.

Some communities may be denominational. In Christianity, for example, Roman Catholics and Anglicans each have their own monastic communities or religious orders, as they are also known. Other communities may be open to any member of the faith as a whole and can be described as inter-denominational. There are also some inter-faith communities in which people from different religions can share their faith together. These communities are concentrated forms of the wider community of all believers. People experience certain benefits from being part of such a group. In the school community, you have a form tutor and head of year to provide you with **pastoral support**. Similarly, in religious communities, there are people who can listen to others and offer help, support, comfort, guidance and counselling. There is also the experience of being with like-minded people who share the same beliefs and values and who, together, can take part in **corporate worship**.

Many religious people also feel they have a number of responsibilities as well. The first of these will usually be to worship God and be a **witness** to the faith in their lives. This is how monks feel, but people in ordinary jobs and in their social life can be an example to others by practising the values of their faith. Honesty, truthfulness, kindness and love can all be shown at any time in any place.

This personal witness can be seen as a form of **evangelism**. An evangelist is someone who spreads the message of a religion to others.

Knocking on people's doors, preaching on the street, holding open meetings or talking directly to people with the intention of converting them, are all forms of evangelism. Missionaries are also evangelists who work abroad, often in hospitals and schools.

Support of voluntary organizations

Service to others is an important part of many people's faith. In some religions, it is a religious duty, or people believe that performing acts of kindness and charity can affect someone's next life. Many individuals simply feel motivated by the needs of others. Support can be given by donating both time and money.

Christian Aid is one of the most well known charities. There is also Muslim Aid. People can support these charities by volunteering their services to organizing fund raising events or to work in their shops. Some actually join the organization and work abroad. Many local faith communities will often organize voluntary work in the wider community. The Salvation Army is famous for its hostels for the homeless and for providing them with meals.

Voluntary work does not necessarily have to be done through religious groups. Secular (non-religious) organizations, such as the Samaritans, have many religious and non-religious people working for them.

❓ Questions

1 How do people show religious commitment through worship?
2 Why do people worship in different ways? Give examples.

💬 For discussion

'Joining a religious community is an escape from reality.' How far do you agree? C2.1a

◆ For research

Organize a visit to a local voluntary organization or invite someone to speak to the class. Find out about the role of full-time and voluntary workers and why they do this sort of thing.

Aim

To understand:

- Christians claims to truth
- how Christians express spirituality in society.

Claims to truth

Christians believe that God is Truth. They also believe that God took human form in the person of Jesus who was full of Truth. In St John's Gospel, Jesus says he is 'the way, the truth and the light' and that no one can reach God the Father except through him. He also promised that after his resurrection he would send the Spirit of Truth from the Father. Christians understand this to be the **Holy Spirit** that is present in the world and now guides them to the Truth.

Religious authorities

The issue of authority has always been a matter of debate in Christianity and has led to divisions in the Church. The Christian Church began with just a few followers of Jesus. As more people became converted to Christianity, these followers began to meet in groups known as churches. Eventually, they grouped together and the Church as an organization developed.

Disagreements about authority

The members of the early Church has to deal with the problems of applying the teachings of Jesus to their everyday lives. They often looked to people within their church to act as spiritual leaders and advisors on moral issues. As time went on, disagreements broke out over various matters of belief, authority and the importance of scriptures.

The first major division in the Church was the Great Schism of 1054. This divided Christianity into the Orthodox Church in the east and the Roman Catholic Church in the west. The Roman Catholic Church continued to accept the supreme authority of the pope as its leader. The Orthodox Church developed a collective leadership.

The next debate came in the sixteenth century. At this time, many Christians were becoming concerned about the power of the pope and how the Church seemed to be moving away from the teachings of Jesus and the authority of the Bible. These protests and the reforms people wanted became known as the **Protestant Reformation**. In Germany, the protests of Martin Luther led to the Lutheran Church being formed. In England, when Henry VIII declared himself head of the Church of England, he began a split with the Roman Catholic Church that would lead to the formation of the Church of England. To this day, the monarch is head of the Church of England, with the Archbishop of Canterbury as head of those who belong to the English Church throughout the world, known as the **Anglican Communion**.

The Church of England developed The Book of Common Prayer, which contains all its services. As time went on, various Anglicans wanted equal freedom to worship in their own way, rather than having to follow or conform to what was in the Prayer Book. Many also had concerns that leaders and traditions were again becoming more important than what they believed to be the Word of God in the Bible. In the following centuries, **denominations** formed that are known as **non-conformist**. Examples are Methodists, Baptists, the United Reformed Church, the Society of Friends (Quakers) and the Salvation Army. They do not have bishops and priests, but in most cases, ministers and a national leader who heads an assembly of ministers and **lay** people. For them, the Bible and the teachings and example of Jesus are the main sources of authority. They believe the Holy Spirit guides their understanding of these and leads them to the Truth.

Sacred writings

Jesus was a Jew who said he came to fulfil the Law and the Prophets. Christians have therefore adopted the Jewish sacred writings as the first part of their Bible known as the Old Testament. They believe this points to Jesus as the **Messiah** or **Christ**. The New Testament contains the gospel (good news) of Jesus according to the saints Matthew, Mark, Luke and John. A book of history, called The Acts of the Apostles, follows these. This contains stories of how the message of Jesus was spread throughout the Mediterranean countries.

The largest section of the New Testament consists of letters, often known as **epistles**, mostly written by St Paul. In these, he explains the faith, sets out beliefs about Jesus and gives rulings on moral issues. Finally, there is The Book of Revelation, a prophecy or foretelling, about the end of the world and the Day of Judgement.

Christians believe the Bible to be the Word of God, although they interpret it differently. Fundamentalists believe the writers were God's messengers and all the words are those of God. There are no errors in their writings and the content is literally true. For liberals, the writers were people who had a special understanding of God's purpose and their faith inspired them to explain God's message. They were only human and therefore capable of making mistakes. Liberals focus on the ideas taught rather than the details of the text, reinterpret them and apply them to modern settings. Others hold views between these two extremes.

Expressing spirituality in society

Individual commitment

Reading the Word of God is the main focus of worship for many Christians, especially among non-conformists. Other Christians use a variety of symbolism and rituals. The celebration of the Liturgy in the Orthodox Church or Mass in the Catholic tradition shows how special clothes, objects and movements can combine to form elaborate ceremonies. The bread, placed on a plate, or **paten**, and the wine poured into a **chalice** as the body and blood of Christ are central to these services. Not all worship takes place publicly. In the home Christians may read the Bible, meditate on or think about specific passages and focus in prayer by using an image, a cross or **crucifix**, or by saying set prayers using a **rosary**.

Support of voluntary organizations

Christians believe their faith is not only about personal spiritual growth but also about expressing the teachings and love of Jesus in a practical way. The Parable of the Good Samaritan (Luke 10: 25–37) and Jesus' words about how people will be judged (Matthew 25: 31–46) are an inspiration for social action. This may range from full-time work in large international organizations to helping in local volunteer groups, whether they have specific religious connections or not.

Membership of a faith community

Most Christians choose to belong to a faith community. For the majority, this means attending their local church or chapel, but some may just belong to prayer groups or attend a house church. In each case, they benefit from sharing their faith, worshipping together and learning from each other. Some Christians choose to devote themselves to God by joining a religious community as a monk or nun. In a monastery, there is a set lifestyle based on the gospel of Christ. Some communities are closed to the outside world, but many are open. Many members perform special types of charity work, such as that done by The Missionaries of Charity, founded by Mother Theresa.

❓ Questions

1 What do Christians believe about the Truth?

2 What are the major divisions in the Church? What is different about their views of authority?

3 How do Christians see the Bible as a source of authority?

4 How do Christians express their spirituality?

💬 For discussion

'A true religion should not have divisions.' How far do you agree? C1.1

◆ For research

1 Use the Internet and work in pairs to find out how Christians express their spirituality in the following ways:

- through the work of an international Christian organization, such as CAFOD or Christian Aid

- through monastic life in The Community of the Resurrection

- through a unique form of Christian witness

Give a talk to the rest of the group about what you have found.
C1, C2; Citizenship 2; IT1.1; WO1, WO2

Aim
To understand:
- Muslims claims to truth
- how Muslims express spirituality in society.

Claims to truth

The basis of Islam is summed up in the **Shahadah**. This states, '*There is no God but Allah and Muhammad is His Messenger.*' Islam sees itself as *the* true religion.

Religious authorities

The worldwide community of Muslims is known as the **ummah**. All Muslims are equal, but locally they are usually led by an **imam**, who is elected to guide the ummah in spiritual matters. He is often seen leading prayers in the mosque, but he also has an important role in looking after the interests of individuals and the community. Differences of opinion about Islamic law (**Shari'ah**) can be settled by a **quadi**, who is a legal expert.

Sacred writings

The **Qur'an** contains the Word of God. It was revealed to Muhammad who recited it to others. It was not written down until after his death. The Qur'an is written in Arabic and translations are not considered true Qur'ans. The Qur'an contains all the beliefs of Islam and Muslims submit themselves to the will of God and try to follow all that the Qur'an requires of them. As it came directly from God and is His final revelation, it is to be obeyed rather than interpreted. Muslims also refer for guidance to the sayings of Muhammad (**Hadith**), which formed part of his whole way of life (**Sunnah**).

Expressing spirituality in society

Individual commitment

The Five Pillars of Islam form the basis of individual commitment. They are:

1 Shahadah – belief in one God and Muhammad as the Messenger of God.
2 Salah – prayer five times a day.
3 **Zakah** – giving to the poor.
4 Sawm – fasting during the month of Ramadan.
5 Hajj – pilgrimage to Makkah.

Prayer is an important part of Muslim life. Muslims must remove their shoes and perform wudu (ritual washing) before they can pray. They will also use a mat so that they are standing on clean ground. In addition to the prayers with set movements (rak'ah), Muslims also say their own prayers (du'a). They may also use beads (subah) to recite the 'Ninety-nine Beautiful Names of Allah' found in the Qur'an. Time will also be set aside for reading the Qur'an.

Support of voluntary organizations

Muslims have a concern and duty to care for each other. This also extends to people in the wider community who are not Muslims. The Qur'an particularly refers to orphans as being in special need of care and many wealthy Muslims and local ummah have set up orphanages around the world.

Membership of a faith community

The ummah provides a sense of security, strength and compassion based on the principle of equality. Equality is shown in the way Muslims treat each other and is symbolized when standing together in prayer and by receiving the same simple funeral. All Muslims know that on the Day of Judgement they must stand before Allah and account for what they have done in this life. Muslims, therefore, help each other in the practice of their faith and support those in need.

? Questions

1 Why is the ummah important in Islam?
2 What do Muslims believe about the Qur'an?

For discussion

'The world would be a better place if everyone believed in a Day of Judgement.' How far do you agree? C1.1

For research

1 Find out what is involved in observing each of the Five Pillars of Islam.

Aim

To understand:

- Jewish claims to truth
- how Jews express spirituality in society.

Claims to truth

Jews believe that some four thousand years ago they were chosen by God to be his people. In return, they promised to worship God and follow his laws. This truth is described in a relationship known as the **covenant**.

Religious authorities

The **rabbi** is a source of knowledge and is an interpreter of the truth in the sacred writings of the **Torah**. Each rabbi is an authority in his or her own right and the interpretation of one rabbi may not be the same as that given by another rabbi.

Judaism does not have a central authority, but is a democratic faith with elected representatives, including local rabbis, and in most parts of the UK there is a chief rabbi to represent the faith. Most Jewish communities will also have a **Bet Din**, which consists of a group of rabbis who give rulings on the most complex or disputed matters. The Bet Din also issues licenses to kosher shops and to kosher goods.

Sacred writings

Truth is revealed to Jews through the scriptures or **TeNaKh**. This has three parts. The first five books is called the Torah and is also known as the Pentateuch. It is the most important because it contains the Law. **Neviim** are books of prophecy and **Ketuvim** are the remaining books of writings. Orthodox Jews take the strictest view about following the scriptures. Conservative, Reform and Liberal or Progressive Jews interpret and adapt them more freely. Jews also recognize the importance of the **Talmud**, a commentary and discussion on how the law is to be followed.

Expressing spirituality in society

Individual commitment

Individual commitment comes from following the Law, observing **tradition**, prayer and family life.

Observing **Shabbat** (the Sabbath) and other festivals reminds Jews of the importance of their faith and history, as does a **mezuzah** placed on the door-posts of the house and wearing symbols of the faith. The **kippah** shows man's relationship to God. **Tefillin** and the **tallit** with **tzitzit** may also be expressions of personal devotion.

Support of voluntary organizations

Helping others through charities, particularly the poor and those who are victims, is a central part of the Jewish faith called **Tzedakah**. The Law requires Jews to give one tenth of their income to the poor. Many Jews also work for charitable organizations or do voluntary work as part of their contribution to community life, which extends to non-Jews as well.

Membership of a faith community

Jews have a strong sense of belonging to a community, both local and international. The synagogue is more than a place where worship, in its narrow sense, takes place. It is a centre where the needs of the community can be made known and be catered for. Children will often attend to learn about their faith and to receive Hebrew lessons to prepare for Bar or Bat Mitzvah. Later, most Jews will marry in the synagogue.

? Questions

1. What is the meaning of all the words in bold?

2. How do Jews express their spirituality?

For discussion

'Helping others is more important than worship.' How far do you agree? C1.1

For research

Working in pairs, find out how Jews express their spirituality in the following ways:

- through the work of organizations
- through signs and symbols
- through the synagogue. C1.2

Claims to truth

Buddhism makes no claims to truth and has no God. The truth is something individuals must find for themselves. In his own life, **Siddattha Gotama**, found a way to **enlightenment**. He believed teachings, such as **The Four Noble Truths**, **The Eightfold Path** and **The Ten Precepts**, might help others along their own path to enlightenment, but they are not laws or commandments.

Religious authorities

People who follow the Buddhist way try to learn from others who are respected for their lifestyle and wisdom, they are not told what to believe or what is true. They also turn to the Three Refuges of the **Buddha**, the **Dhamma** and the **Sangha**. The Buddha's life is an example of reaching enlightenment. The Dhamma is made up of his teachings. The Sangha is the whole Buddhist community, but often refers to those who have become monks or nuns or who are respected teachers. Their authority is only what is given to them by those who learn from them.

Sacred writings

The main Buddhist scriptures, the **Tipitaka Sutras**, have three sections. They cover the codes of behaviour, stories of the life of Buddha and his teachings, and commentaries on the teachings. Buddhists study these writings and learn from them. They have authority only in the sense that they relate to the Buddha and his teachings and provide a basis for living that Buddhists can interpret themselves.

Expressing spirituality in society

Individual commitment

The sacred writings are also recited, along with chants and special words, known as **mantras**.

In some forms of Buddhism, these mantras are placed in prayer wheels that are spun to remind people of the teachings and to send out positive influences. Statues of the Buddha often serve as a focus for devotion. Other items, such as flowers, candles, incense, food, water and bells, also have symbolic meaning. As well as making offerings, Buddhists usually spend time in meditation. This can take many forms, but is intended to produce inner calm and take people further along the path to enlightenment. A string of beads, know as juzu or mala, is used in some types of meditation.

Support of voluntary organizations

The Buddhist understanding of life focuses on the existence of suffering. Many Buddhists believe they have a responsibility to overcome suffering in a practical way, as well as a spiritual way. They also believe in **karma**, that what they do in this life will affect their rebirth. Working for voluntary organizations is part of what has become known as **Engaged Buddhism**, because it engages people in doing good for the community.

Membership of a faith community

For many Buddhists the idea of belonging is a form of attachment, something they would usually try to avoid. However, most Buddhists belong to spiritual communities in the form of their local temple. Some Buddhists may choose to join a monastery for a time. Others give their whole lives to being a monk or a nun.

? Questions

1. How do Buddhists learn about their faith?
2. Why do you think Buddhists respect the teachings of other religions?

For discussion

Buddhism is an eastern religion that is popular with many people in the west. Why do you think this is? C1.1

For research

1. Find out the meaning of symbolic objects used in Buddhist devotions.
2. Use the Internet to find out more about Buddhist teachings.

Aim

To understand:

- Hindus claims to truth
- how Hindus express spirituality in society.

Claims to truth

Truth for Hindus lies in belief in one God (Brahman), also referred to as the Universal Spirit or Ultimate Reality. The meaning of Brahman is beyond human understanding and can be represented in many forms.

Religious authorities

Tradition is seen as a source of authority for some Hindus. However, it is possible for Hindus to worship different aspects of Brahman, such as Shiva or Visnu, or other Gods, such as Ganesha. So all Hindus would not accept the same tradition. There are gurus (teachers) and sadhus (holy men) whose authority comes from being respected by others. Most Hindus simply believe and practise what has been passed on from one generation to another.

Sacred writings

Many sacred writings have influenced Hinduism. None can be thought of as having authority in the sense of being *the* holy book. **Shruti** scriptures are regarded as the more important because Hindus believe God revealed them to the holy men who passed them on before being written down. They include the Vedas and the Upanishads. **Smriti** are human accounts of God's teachings and contain some of the most popular stories. The Mahabharata, the Ramayana, the Laws of Manu and the Puranas are in this group. Together they cover all aspects of life.

Expressing spirituality in society

Individual commitment

Most personal devotion takes place in the home. Hindus generally have a shrine where it is customary for the women of the house to perform **puja**. This can involve elaborate rituals, using items that appeal to the different senses, such as a bell, a lamp, flowers, food and incense. Hindus may also pray together and practise various forms of meditation, including yoga and the use of mantras.

Support of voluntary organizations

Hindus must follow what they believe to be their **dharma** (duty). This can be likened to the idea of conscience. They also believe in **karma**, that what they say and do in this life will have consequences for their next life. Hindus must also act according to their **varna** (caste) and ashrama (the stage they have reached in life). To these must be added the belief in **artha**, to achieve wealth by honest means and to take care of the needs of the family and community. This complex set of beliefs provides the motivation for Hindus to support voluntary organizations.

Membership of a faith community

Hinduism can be described as a way of interpreting life. In India, some people may spend time in an **ashram** or religious community to study their faith more deeply or devote themselves to a particular lifestyle. In the UK, where Hindus are one of many minority groups, there is an identifiable faith community. Most Hindus can trace their families back to India or Nepal. Being a Hindu, therefore, is more than just belonging to a religion, it is at the heart of a people's culture and identity. For this reason, temples in the UK often serve as a focus, not only for worship, but as a centre of support and security for the whole Hindu community.

? Questions

1 What are the disadvantages of having no sources of authority in a religion?

2 What do you think is meant by having a sense of duty?

3 In what ways do you think the Hindu community supports its members in the UK?

For discussion

'Worshipping in the home keeps a family together.' How far do you agree? C2.1a

For research

Find out how puja is performed in the home and the meaning of the items used. C2.2

Aim

To understand:

- Sikhs claims to truth
- how Sikhs express spirituality in society.

Claims to truth

Sikhs believe in one God. What God is like is beyond human understanding and nothing can adequately describe him. The first thing said in the **Mool Mantra** is that His name is Eternal Truth. In the scriptures, He is referred to by hundreds of different names, but True One is frequently used.

Religious authorities

Authority in Sikhism rests on the idea of Guruship. The word **Guru** refers to God, who is the ultimate authority, the ten human Gurus, who taught God's message and the sacred writings of the **Guru Granth Sahib**. There is also the Guruship of the **Khalsa**, which can make decisions about the faith. Sikhs turn to these for guidance and instruction in all aspects of life. In the **Gurdwara**, the Guru Granth Sahib is read by a **granthi**, but can be interpreted only by a **giani**, who will be knowledgeable about it.

Sacred writings

Following the death of Guru Gobind Singh, the Guru Granth Sahib became the living Guru. It is the highest source of authority as it contains the teachings of the ten Gurus and the work of other inspired writers. There is also a collection of writings by Guru Gobind Singh known as the **Dasam Granth**. The best known part of this work is the **Jap**, which is used daily in worship. Although not a sacred writing, a code of conduct, the **Reht Maryada**, was put together in the last century.

Expressing spirituality in society

Individual commitment

Sikhs are required to constantly remember God. This can be done through worship and service to others. Worship can only be fully carried out in the gurdwara, because that is where the Guru

Granth Sahib is kept. Few Sikhs have a Guru Granth Sahib in their homes, as they need to provide a separate upstairs room and proper respect. They will probably have a **gutka**, which contains hymns from the Guru Granth Sahib. This can be used in private devotion in addition to the morning and evening prayers in the home.

Support of voluntary organizations

Sikhs believe there is no worship without giving selfless service to others (**sewa**) and a tenth of their wealth is given to those less fortunate (**daswandh**). They also believe that they should share what they have with others (**vand chhakna**) and that what they do in this life will affect their new life (**karma**). These beliefs form the basis of Sikh support for voluntary organizations.

Membership of a faith community

The sense of community is very strong among Sikhs. Since the division of their homeland, Punjab, in 1947, many Sikhs have settled in other parts of the world, such as the UK. The gurdwara has become not only a place of worship, but also a cultural and social centre that caters for the wider needs of the community and supports them in their lives. Here Sikhs can express their faith and, in particular, demonstrate their belief in the equality of all people by sharing the **langar** meal.

? Questions

1. What are the advantages and disadvantages of having clear sources of authority?

2. How do Sikhs express their faith in practical ways?

📑 For discussion

'Worship without service to others has little meaning.' How far do you agree? C2.1a

◆ For research

1. How do Sikhs show respect for the Guru Granth Sahib?

2. Use the Internet to find out about the work of a Sikh community centre. IT2.1

Aim

To review a summary of the important issues concerning nature and expression and to study some exam questions.

Now that you have considered the difficult religious issues on nature and expression, it is time to see if you can answer the type of question that will appear in exams. Before you do so, have a look at the factfile summary to check how much you know.

Factfile summary

I need to make sure that I:

○ • understand the meaning of scientific, historical, moral and spiritual truth, the differences between them and the problems associated with them.

○ • understand the difference between evidence, proof, probability and certainty.

• understand the meaning of belief and trust.

○ • understand the meaning of reason and experience in relation to faith and their limitations.

○ • understand the idea of spirituality and the words and expressions used in relation to spirituality.

○ • understand what is meant by religious authorities and sacred writings, how they can be interpreted differently.

○ • understand what is meant by conscience.

• understand how people can express individual commitment through symbolism, piety and creativity.

○ • understand why people support voluntary organizations and the different ways they can help.

• understand what is meant by membership of a faith community and the different types of communities.

Exam questions

Read the following statements and then answer the following questions.

Statement A: I'm religious. My holy book and my conscience tell me what is true.

Statement B: The only truth is what science can prove. Belonging to a religion is a waste of time.

Statement C: There's more to life than science can prove. I'm not religious, but I think we all have a spiritual side.

1 Look at Statement A.

   a Give an example of a holy book.

   b What is meant by conscience?   [3 marks]

2 Look at Statement B.

   a How does science prove that something is true?

   b How would a religious believer argue against the idea that 'belonging to a religion is a waste of time'?   [8 marks]

3 Look at Statement C.

   Explain why it might be said that all people have a spiritual side.   [4 marks]

4 'The only truth is what science can prove.' Do you agree? Give reasons for your answer, showing that you have thought about more than one point of view. Refer to religious teachings in your answer.   [5 marks]

The start of life

Aim
To investigate:
- when life begins
- the idea of pre-existence
- who is responsible for life.

Modern developments in medicine, medical research and medical techniques have caused many people to be concerned about the morality of what is being done or what is being planned. Key questions include:

- When does life begin?
- Who is responsible for life?
- Should embryos be used for research?

There are several stages in the development of a baby.

- The just-fertilized ovum is called a **zygote.**
- After five to seven days of cell division, the **blastocyst** develops.
- Twelve to fourteen days after fertilization it becomes implanted into the wall of the womb. Then it is called an **embryo.**
- When all the organs have developed it is called a **foetus.** This takes about eleven weeks after fertilization has taken place.

When does life begin?

- **Fertilization**
  At the moment when the sperm fertilizes the egg, a new life, distinct from that of the father and mother, begins with a unique genetic code. Those who believe life starts at fertilization see the embryo as a human being and argue that this deserves all the rights of a born child. Experiments that put the embryo at risk are not acceptable. They believe that embryo research might have the potential to help the human race, but ethically it is wrong if it results in the death of the embryo or carries a significant risk of causing damage.

- **Implantation**
  Some suggest that life begins at implantation. This is the point when the blastocyst is attached to the womb and the woman becomes a mother in a fuller sense. It is estimated that 30–50 per cent of the fertilized cells may be lost before this stage. These are aborted naturally by the mother.

- **Primitive steak**
  After about fourteen days, the first anatomical feature, the **primitive steak**, appears in the position in which the backbone will later develop. Until this point, we cannot tell if the embryo is going to be one or two individuals because splitting can take place. Separation can happen about the time of the eight cell division, immediately before, during or immediately after implantation.

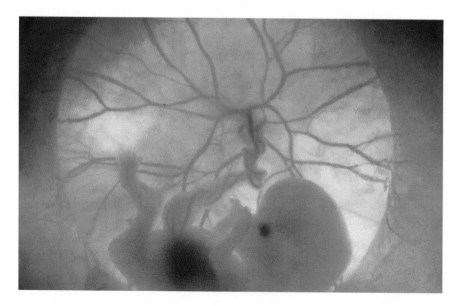

A foetus in the womb

- **Movement or heart beat**

  Others argue that when the mother first feels the baby move or at the first heart beat, then life begins. Movement is seen as an indication of some form of awareness and the ability to feel pleasure or pain is of real moral significance. Studies show that movement takes place as early as six weeks after fertilization (although the mother is not aware of it at this stage).

- **Viability**

  Another idea is that life begins when the foetus is **viable**. This means that if it was born it could survive. The problem with this idea is that the point at which the foetus can survive outside the mother's body varies according to the state of medical technology. 40 years ago it was generally accepted that a baby born more than two months premature could not survive. Now, thanks to modern medical techniques, even babies born three and a half months premature have survived.

- **Birth**

  Some people believe that life only truly begins when the baby is born.

Does it matter?

Those who take the view that the fertilized ovum is not a human life (but has the potential to become a human being) may argue that it may be justifiable to perform experiments on embryos if it helps the human race. For example, before 14 days there is no organ structure or even a primitive brain, just a collection of cells that could divide into two and produce twins. A cell could be taken in the very early stages of pregnancy to check for disease. If it was found to be abnormal, the pregnancy could be ended.

Is there such a thing as a pre-existence?

Is it possible that we pre-existed – that some part of ourselves existed before we were conceived? Many believe that we may have had previous lives and been reborn over and over again. This might have been in a lower life form or as a human being.

This idea is known as reincarnation or rebirth. In Buddhism, Hinduism and Sikhism, it is believed that rebirth may occur where the fruits of our good and bad actions (karma) in the previous life are experienced. They believe that this continues until the cycle of rebirths is broken and liberation (freedom) is achieved.

Who is responsible for life?

Many religious believers argue that God is responsible for all life, but Buddhists or atheists do not believe in God. The answer to this question is a critical one in the debate concerning medical research. If God or a Supreme Power is responsible, then the question arises, 'What right has a scientist to interfere in the production of children or in the alteration of genes?' What responsibilities do parents and doctors have?

? Questions

1 Why is it important to establish when life begins?

2 Briefly describe the arguments that could be used to support the idea that life begins at:
  a fertilization
  b implantation
  c appearance of the primitive steak
  d the first heart beat or movement
  e viability
  f birth.

For discussion

1 Who do you think is responsible for life? Give reasons. C2.1a

2 Do you think that it is possible that we pre-existed? Give reasons.

For research

Investigate the stages of development from a fertilized egg to a fully formed foetus. When do you think life begins? C1.2

Infertility and fertility treatment

Aim
To investigate ways in which modern developments in medical science may help infertile couples to have children.

Fertility treatment

According to Child, the National Infertility Support Network, one in six couples in Britain suffer from infertility. Thousands of childless couples would love to have a baby and turn to fertility treatment. Currently, about 27 000 couples receive fertility treatment each year. Statistics show that there is only a one in six chance of the treatment resulting in a pregnancy. The treatment is expensive, an average of about £3000 an attempt, and this is not usually covered by the National Health Service.

The use of fertility treatment raises many moral questions. For example, who should be helped? At what age is a couple too old to have children?

What forms of fertility treatment are acceptable? Who has the right to make these decisions?

There has been an example of a 60-year-old woman giving birth. Should there be an age limit?

Types of fertility treatment

AIH
Artificial insemination with the husband's sperm is when artificial methods are used to put the husband's sperm into the woman.

AID
AID is when the mother's egg is fertilized with a donor's sperm because the male partner is infertile, or if a single woman wishes to have a child. Although this is done extensively in the selective breeding of farm animals, many oppose this technique being used on humans. One obvious problem is that the child will not know its biological father. Some religious believers regard the use of a donor's sperm as being the same as adultery.

Thousands of childless couples use fertility treatment in order to have a baby

IVF

In vitro fertilization (IVF) is where the sperm and egg are collected from the man and the woman and put together to achieve fertilization in a test tube. This procedure has led to the term 'test tube babies', the first of whom, Louise Brown, was born in 1978. In 2001, one in 80 children born are the result of IVF treatment.

Further improvement of IVF techniques has required continued experimentation and many embryos have been destroyed in these experiments. Embryos can now be frozen and stored for many years before being thawed and implanted in the womb.

There was such concern over the way that humankind now appeared to be able to 'manufacture' babies, that the government introduced The Human Fertilization and Embryology Act, 1990. It sets out regulations on:

* research using human embryos

* the storage of eggs, sperm and embryos

* fertility treatment that uses donated eggs or sperm (for example, AID), or embryos that are created outside the body (IVF).

Surrogacy

Surrogacy is when a woman has a baby for another woman. She may become pregnant by sperm donation from either the father or another man. For many, surrogacy is the only alternative to childlessness. They may have already tried to adopt a child or have spent thousands of pounds on unsuccessful medical treatment.

Some people saw surrogacy as a way to make large sums of money from those who were desperate to have a child, so the government passed an act to regulate it. The Surrogacy Arrangements Act, 1985:

* made it a criminal offence to advertise surrogacy in any way

* made it illegal for payments to be made to a company or agency who assisted in the surrogacy arrangements. It did not ban payment to the surrogate mother.

The Human Fertilization and Embryology Act, 1990 also covered surrogacy. It said that:

* The child must be genetically related to at least one of the commissioning couple (that is, using the egg or sperm of either parent).

* The surrogate mother cannot be forced to give up her child at the end of the pregnancy.

* The commissioning couple must both be over 18 and married to each other.

* No money other than expenses must be paid in respect of the surrogacy arrangement.

Six weeks after birth the intended parents can apply for a Parental Order. This will give them full and permanent parental rights over the child. Problems may arise if the surrogate mother wishes to keep the child or if at a later date the child suddenly finds out that he or she has a surrogate mother.

❓ Questions

1 Explain what is meant by:

  a AIH

  b AID

  c IVF

  d surrogacy.

2 Describe the main points of:

  a The Surrogacy Arrangements Act, 1985

  b The Human Fertilization Embryology Act, 1990.

💬 For discussion

1 Do you think that there should be an age limit for couples who wish to have fertility treatment?

2 'We shouldn't mess with nature.' How far do you agree?

3 How would you feel if you suddenly discovered that you were a 'test tube' baby, or that you had a surrogate mother? Citizenship 2b

◆ For research

Find out about COTS (Childlessness Overcome Through Surrogacy) by researching their website. Make notes on your findings. IT2.1

Genetic engineering

Aim

To investigate:

- the make up of the human cell
- different types of cloning
- the debate about cloning humans.

Can you imagine designing the genes for your children? It may soon be possible to choose a child's sex, height, eye, hair and skin colour, intelligence, athleticism and make-up. Imagine designing a child so that he or she will be ideally suited for a particular job, such as a doctor, engineer or artist. Are we ready for the creation of super humans? Is this a nightmare scenario or a leap forward for the human race?

At the centre of the trillions of cells that make up each human being is a code, which we call genes. It is made from DNA (deoxyribonucleic acid) and it contains instructions for the substances that create our bodies. The name given to all these genes is the human genome. The genome has been likened to a recipe book or a blueprint for each individual person. Recently, scientists have claimed to have mapped or worked out what makes up the human genome.

Many people claim that the discovery of the map of the human genome will have a tremendous impact on tackling illness. Faulty genes that cause disease can be genetically modified. This would prevent diseases from developing, for example, in families where there has been a history of cystic fibrosis or cancer.

Many moral and ethical questions arise as a result. Is it right for humans to alter human genes? Is it 'playing God' to start altering aspects of human make-up? Is there a difference between repairing genetic damage and trying to make genetic improvements to humans?

Cloning

Cloning is the production of genetically identical (sharing the same set of genes) individuals.

There are two very different ways that this happens. Firstly, there is **embryo cloning**. This involves the removal of one or more cells from an embryo and encouraging the cell(s) to develop into a separate embryo. This type of cloning has been carried out with several types of animals.

Secondly, there is **therapeutic cloning**. This involves taking the DNA out of an embryo and replacing it with DNA from another individual. The embryo is killed in the process, but the stem cells may then be grown into a replacement heart, liver or skin, and so on. This process is still being developed, but if it is successful perfectly matched replacement organs could become available to those who are seriously ill. There would be no danger of the body rejecting the transplant because the organ's DNA would match the patient's DNA.

Issues

- Therapeutic cloning raises the issue when does life begin? If it starts at conception is it right to first alter an embryo and then have it killed?

- Scientists are now claiming that they will soon be able to clone a human. Dr Ian Wilmut, who cloned Dolly the sheep, said that it took 277 times to get a perfect animal. The first 276 attempts resulted in many malformed animals. Would an attempt to create a human clone result in deformed humans?

- Cloning might lead to 'designer babies', as parents could choose the sex of their offspring. In the wrong hands it could have terrible consequences. In Germany, during World War II, the Nazis, who believed in the superiority of the Germanic races, sent millions of Jews, gypsies and handicapped people to their deaths in the concentration camps.

So these issues have led to a number of arguments against cloning.

Arguments against the cloning of humans

- Cloning is 'playing God' and interfering in nature. Dividing a fertilized ovum would be to interfere with God's intention.

- Cloning denies the 'sanctity of human life'.

- The clone may not have a soul. If a soul enters the body at conception and the fertilized ovum is a human being, then a cloned embryo may not have one.

Will we create a super human or a monster?

- Life starts at conception so the many cloned zygotes, which die as a result of the process of cloning, are lost human beings. This is murdering unborn children.

- Experiments with human cloning will undoubtedly result in malformed clones, as happened before the successful cloning of Dolly the sheep.

Whatever the rights and wrongs, many governments, including the UK, have banned human cloning as being morally and ethically unacceptable.

Arguments for the cloning of humans

- Cloning creates life from life and is just an extension of IVF (*in vitro* fertilization). It is no more 'playing God' than other fertility treatments.

- It cannot be proven that a soul exists, as it has never been detected by any measurement. No one questions whether twins have souls.

- Changing a single two-cell form of life into two one-cell forms of life and discarding any unwanted cells is not murder. The cells may have the potential to become humans, but at this very early stage true life has not begun.

- Cloning might help to improve the human race and speed up the process of evolution.

? Questions

1. What are genes and why are they important?
2. How might human genetic engineering be used to help the human race?
3. What is meant by embryo cloning and therapeutic cloning?

For discussion

1. Are we right to be tampering with human nature?
2. Organize a debate to discuss 'It is "playing God" to try to clone a human being'. WO2.1

For research

Research the websites on human cloning and use the information to write a short play based on what might happen if human gene therapy or cloning went wrong. Citizenship 2a

Medical research and practice

> ### Aim
> To investigate:
> - transplant surgery
> - blood transfusions.

Transplant surgery

On 3 December 1967, the first successful heart transplant took place. Dr Christiaan Barnard's patient, at a hospital in Cape Town, South Africa, lived for 18 days after the operation. Six months later in Essex, Fred West became the first British person to have a heart transplant. The operation at the National Heart Hospital was described as technically a great success, but Mr West died 46 days later.

The causes of these deaths was the complex biological problem of tissue rejection, but a drug (Cyclosporin), developed from a fungus found in Norway during the 1970s, has vastly improved the patient survival rate. Now, more than 300 heart transplants are carried out each year in Britain alone and it is estimated that the patients have a 60 per cent chance of living for more than ten years. It remains a long and costly operation and expensive anti-rejection drugs have to be taken for the rest of the person's life. In addition, many people wait in vain for a suitable donor to become available.

Transplant operations save or improve the lives of thousands of people each year as organs like hearts, kidneys, livers or corneas are replaced. The lack of organs is a major problem, with about 5000 patients in Britain currently waiting for a suitable donor.

Of major concern has been the discovery that some hospitals have been taking organs from people who have died and have stored them or used them for medical research without first obtaining permission from the dead person's relatives. Figures released in January 2001 by the Department of Health revealed that 25 hospitals and medical schools held more than 500 organs, body parts and still births/pre-viable foetuses. The Royal Liverpool Children's hospital held 6900.

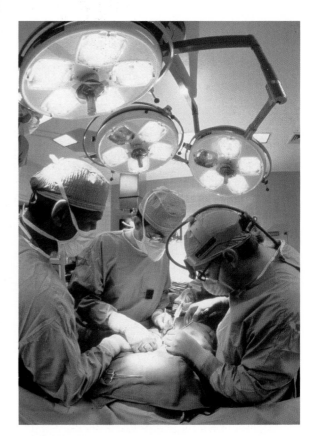

Transplant operations save or improve the lives of thousands of people each year

Scientists have recently been investigating the possibility of using pigs to help overcome the donor shortage. Transplanting genetically modified pig hearts and lungs would enable many more people to be given the organs they require. Questions arise concerning whether it is morally right to use animals in this way. Some scientists are also very worried that viruses found in pigs may be transmitted to humans and prove to be very dangerous.

Blood

In 1628, William Harvey discovered that blood circulated around the body. Richard Lower, using animals, carried out the first successful blood transfusion in 1655. Experiments on humans proved to be more of a problem because the people given the blood kept dying. It was just over a hundred years ago that it was discovered that blood comes in four main types or groups – O, A, B and AB. Giving a patient the wrong blood group was the reason for the earlier deaths.

Group O is the most common blood group and around 10 000 units of blood are needed each day in this country. This is collected from nearly two million donors.

Blood transfusions

Blood transfusions are common after people have lost blood in accidents or in operations. It is said that bloodless surgery increases the risk of death by between 35–40 per cent. It is possible to carry out operations using plasma products and blood recycled from the patient's own body, but the risks are much greater.

In November 1999, Beverley Matthews, a 33-year-old mother from Stockport, refused to have a blood transfusion because of her religious beliefs. She had an infection that was causing her blood to start destroying itself. Doctors hoped that by giving her the blood transfusion it would give the antibiotics time to work and for the poisons to clear. She and her family refused the treatment and she died hours later. As a Jehovah's Witness, she believed it wrong to have the transfusion and so her last chance of survival was gone.

In the case of Marina Ferreira, a different decision was taken. Marina, aged 65, was admitted to hospital suffering from pneumonia, heart and kidney failure and internal bleeding. Her two elder daughters, Rolando Ferreira and Xinia Turnbull, both Roman Catholics, wanted the doctors to give a blood transfusion to save her life. Marina and her youngest daughter, as Jehovah's Witnesses,

opposed blood transfusions. After great argument, Marina was given a blood transfusion. On her recovery Marina sued the hospital and said that what her elder children did was equal to rape.

? Questions

1 What is meant by transplant surgery?
2 Why did the first heart transplant patients survive for only a short time?
3 Why do you think that there is a shortage of available organs for transplantation?
4 Do you think that it is morally right to use animal organs in transplant surgery? Give reasons.
5 Explain the significance of blood groups in blood transfusions. Give reasons.

For discussion

Discuss the cases of Beverley Matthews and Marina Ferreira. What advice would you have given them and their families? Give reasons. Citizenship 3a

For research

Use the Internet to find and make notes of some examples of people whose lives have been saved by having blood transfusions. Citizenship 2a IT2.1

Christianity

Christians believe that God is the creator of life and that humans have a special relationship with him.

> 'Then God said, "And now we will make human beings; they will be like us and resemble us".'
>
> (Genesis 1: 26)

Life is special and sacred. Psalm 139: 13 and 15 suggests that God not only creates us but knows us while we are developing in the womb.

Fertility treatment and surrogacy

Christians regard children as a gift from God. Matthew 19: 13–15 shows that Jesus had a special affection for the young, as he was never too tired to give the children his attention. A purpose of Christian marriage is to provide a stable and loving environment for the raising of a family.

A range of views exists concerning the use of fertility treatment.

- The Roman Catholic Church does not support the creation of spare embryos, which are either thrown away or used for experimentation. As Roman Catholics believe that life begins when the egg is fertilized, such actions are the same as killing human life. Neither do they agree with AID, IVF and surrogacy. Roman Catholics believe that every person has a right to have two biological parents.

- Others including Methodists, Baptists, Anglicans and the Salvation Army, accept AIH and IVF, but not AID. They argue that AIH and IVF are all right because the parents are married and how the pregnancy began is not important.

- Christians do not support AID or IVF, where donated sperm or donated ova are used, because it is like a third person becoming involved in the marriage.

- Surrogacy is considered wrong for similar reasons and, for example, Anglicans believe that it is wrong to pay a woman to bear a child for another.

Embryology, transplant surgery and blood transfusions

Many Christians believe that embryo research threatens the sanctity of human life. They oppose the idea of freezing embryos to use later, even if they can be used to create replacement cells to help people suffering from diseases like Parkinson's and diabetes.

> 'The human embryo has the right to proper respect. Test tube babies are real babies not simple embryos to be manipulated, frozen or left to die.'
>
> (The Roman Catholic Truth Society, 1985)

Others who believe that life begins at a later stage in the pregnancy support research providing that safeguards are in place. A Church of England report in 1994 said:

> 'We support the recommendation that research, under license, be permitted on embryos up to 14 days old and agree that embryos should not be created just for scientific research.'

Most Christian denominations support organ, blood and tissue donation. The Brethren Conference in 1993 passed the following resolution:

> 'We have the opportunity to help others out of the love for Christ, through the donation of organs and tissues.'

The Greek Orthodox Church is not opposed to organ donation provided it is used to better human life. The organs may be used for transplant surgery, or for research that is designed to lead to the prevention of disease or improvements in treatment.

Transplants and blood transfusions are acceptable to Roman Catholics. Donation of organs and blood are seen as acts of charity.

Some denominations, for example, The Society of Friends (Quakers) and Pentecostalists, do not have an official policy on organ donation but allow each individual member to make up his or her own mind.

Jehovah's Witnesses allow transplant surgery but not blood transfusions. This results from the command in Leviticus 17: 10–11, not to eat blood, because *'The life of everything is in the blood'*. This means that all blood must be removed from the organs and tissues before being transplanted.

Genetic engineering

Many Christians are worried that genetic engineering may make basic and irreversible changes to God's sacred creation – humans. Roman Catholics believe that there are borders that we cannot cross without becoming destroyers of creation.

Others argue that God is the creator and that His work is ongoing. As we are created in God's image we are 'co-creators' with God, and human genetic engineering is our contribution to this. Human genetic engineering can be used in a positive way to make the world more just and to help everyone to have good health.

Methodists accept genetic engineering if it is used as a means of healing diseases, but are concerned about what might happen if the wrong people start to use it.

Cloning

There is no single Christian view on cloning humans, but it is not acceptable to most. The Anglican Church, like most denominations, does not oppose cloning animals but believes that this new scientific development must be used responsibly. Most Anglicans argue that the cloning of humans is not desirable. Roman Catholics state that to use technology to copy a human being is a threat to our individuality. God has given us all a uniqueness that He has given to no one else.

Some Christians argue that cloning humans risks making children products of technology rather than gifts created in love. How a human clone would be treated is a real concern, for example, the idea of creating a human clone to use for spare parts is totally opposed.

Some Christian thinkers are urging the Church not to rule out human cloning completely because it is a very new scientific development. They believe that if cloning was carefully controlled then there might be benefits to the human race.

❓ Questions

1 Who do Christians believe is responsible for life?
2 Why are children important to Christians?
3 Explain Christian beliefs concerning AIH, AID, IVF and surrogacy.
4 Explain Christian views about embryology, transplant surgery and blood transfusions.
5 Why are many Christians opposed to cloning humans?

💬 For discussion

'Christians should support research into genetic engineering as it will provide a cure for so many diseases.' Do you agree? Give reasons.
Citizenship 1f

◆ For research

Are scientists going one step too far? Use the Internet to find and record Christian views about cloning and human genetic engineering. IT2.1a

Aim
To understand Muslim beliefs concerning:
- fertility treatment and surrogacy
- medical research and practice.

Muslims believe that Allah creates human life and provides the gift of children.

'He gives daughters to whom He will and sons to whom He pleases.'

(Surah 42: 49)

Life begins with the fusion of the sperm and the egg. Life and the spirit are not the same and some Muslims believe that the soul is breathed into the foetus on the 120th day of pregnancy.

Fertility treatment and surrogacy

In Islam, procreation comes from a marriage contract between two people – the husband and the wife. Certain fertility treatments are allowed if the married couple need help. These include IVF – the test tube fertilization of the husband's sperm and the wife's egg, and AIH – the artificial insemination of the woman with the sperm of her husband. AID is forbidden because to use sperm from an unknown donor is seen as similar to committing adultery.

Surrogacy is opposed because *'No one can be their mother except those who gave them birth'* (Qur'an 58: 2). Muslims may marry up to four wives (providing the state laws allow it) so surrogacy is seen as unnecessary.

Embryology, transplant surgery and blood transfusions

Islamic medical ethics are based on the sanctity of human life. Muslims forbid the conception or the deliberate abortion of a foetus for the sole purpose of taking its tissues for medical research. Embryos left over from IVF treatment may be used.

Muslims allow transplant surgery, but safeguards must be in place.

'If anyone has saved a life, it would be as if he has saved the life of the whole of mankind.'

(Qur'an 5: 32)

It is haram (forbidden) to sell body parts. The organs must be donated and permission must be given by the donor or a relative to receive the body part. Organs may not be removed from a dead person unless a will has been made giving permission. Organs from animals, including pigs, may be used.

Muslims allow blood donation and transfusion, but only in cases of genuine need. Under normal circumstances, Muslims believe that it is wrong to sell one's blood or to pay the blood donor.

Genetic engineering and cloning

Muslims allow research into genetic engineering and the cloning of animals or plants. There is concern over the possibility of cloning a human being. Human cloning may undermine family ties and social order. Questions arise about the individuality and identity of the cloned person. Muslims oppose taking a living cell from an individual and the placing of it into another cell which has had its nucleus removed. Most Muslims are against human cloning, but some argue that it may be necessary to make some exceptions in the future. The use of cloning in IVF as an aid to fertility, strictly within the bounds of marriage, may prove to be acceptable to both Sunni and Shi'i Muslims.

? Questions
1. Who, according to Islam, provides the gift of children?
2. Explain the Muslim beliefs concerning fertility treatments.
3. What do Muslims believe about embryology, transplant surgery and blood transfusions?
4. Explain Muslim views about human genetic engineering and cloning.

For discussion
'A family is incomplete without children.' Do you agree? Give reasons. Citizenship 2c

Aim

To understand Jewish beliefs concerning:
* fertility treatment and surrogacy
* medical research and practice.

Jews believe in the sanctity of life and that all life comes from and is created by God. Each person is unique and valuable and life is a gift from God. He knows us before we are born (Psalm 139: 13 and 15) and gives us a purpose for our lives (Jeremiah 1: 5). In Judaism, children are regarded as a blessing and procreation (having children) is encouraged within marriage.

Fertility treatment and surrogacy

For childless couples, artificial insemination with the husband's sperm (AIH) is allowed. AID is not acceptable but IVF is permitted. The idea of surrogacy is not acceptable to Jews, as the idea of motherhood is very important in Judaism. The Torah commands: *'Honour your father and mother.'* With surrogacy, who is the mother – the genetic mother (egg donor) or the birth mother (the one who actually gives birth)?

Embryology, transplant surgery and blood transfusions

Judaism encourages lawful medical research and development. Jews believe that embryos outside the body have no moral status. They accept using spare embryos from IVF treatment or aborted foetuses for use in developing treatments, though there is opposition to buying and selling stem cells.

Organ donation is encouraged. Many Jews believe that it is their duty to donate an organ, such as a kidney, if it will save another person's life. Some Jews support the taking of some organs from brain dead patients and using them to save lives. Included is the donation of corneas, as the restoring of a person's eyesight is regarded as a life-saving operation. Judaism does not oppose the use of organs from animals.

In Judaism, saving a life is paramount, so it is a mitzvah (good deed) and an obligation to replace lost blood by transfusion if the situation requires it. Jews are encouraged to be blood donors.

Genetic engineering

Knowledge of the human genome (all the genes that make up a human being) promises to lead to medical developments that will have great benefits in the fight against disease. The danger lies in using it to 'play God'. Jews do not support the selective breeding of humans or the engineering of supposedly 'desirable' characteristics, such as choosing the colour of a child's eyes.

Cloning

There is no clear agreement yet in Jewish law regarding human cloning. The Torah says that originally man and woman were one being and that God separated them after creation. When a man and woman marry, they come together to form the original whole (Genesis 2: 23–4). God instructed them (Genesis 1: 28) to unite and to *'Have many children'*. Does cloning interfere with this idea of creating new life together or is it another way of ensuring that our descendants will *'live all over the earth and bring it under their control'* (Genesis 1: 28)? The Torah says that we should use knowledge to cure and prolong life, and the use of cloning to produce replacement organs may not be controversial. To clone human life goes beyond that. Some would argue that this is attempting to 'play God'.

? Questions

1 Why do Jews believe that all life is valuable?
2 How are children viewed in Judaism?
3 Explain which forms of fertility treatment are allowed in Judaism.
4 What do Jews believe about embryology, blood transfusions and transplant surgery?
5 Explain Jewish attitudes towards human genetic engineering and cloning.

For discussion

'A marriage that is truly blessed by God produces children.' Do you agree? Give reasons.
Citizenship 2b

Buddhists believe that being born in human form is rare and is very precious. All living things are caught in **samsara** (the cycle of birth, death and rebirth). Life has already begun before conception in an earlier existence.

Fertility treatment and surrogacy

Religious pressure is not put on Buddhists to marry and have children. Many choose to become monks or nuns. Each individual has the personal choice regarding whether or not to use IVF, other forms of medical help or surrogacy to start a family. There are no grounds in Buddhism to say that it is either immoral or irreligious to have fertility treatment. Conception can take place either naturally or artificially.

Embryology, transplant surgery and blood transfusions

Buddhists ask about the motives and intentions behind the new medical research and technological possibilities. The Buddhist aim is to end suffering, as shown in the care of the sick. According to the Vinaya, the Buddha himself said:

> *'Whoever, O monks, would nurse me, he should nurse the sick.'*
>
> (Zysk, 1991: 41)

Buddhists consider embryos to be living beings, but many today believe that the embryo does not fully embody all five **skandhas** (form, feelings, perceptions, thoughts and consciousness). Most Buddhists argue that, as life begins at conception, the use of embryos in scientific experiments should be approached with extreme caution as it is wrong to kill or harm any living thing. Others say that, if the embryo is not yet a fully embodied person, then the karmic consequences of such action is even less than killing animals.

Buddhists do not oppose transplant surgery or blood transfusions and they believe that organ donation is a matter of individual conscience. Acts of compassion are highly valued. Buddhists believe that it is important for those who wish to donate organs to inform their families or permission will not be given for their use in transplantation.

Genetic engineering and cloning

Buddhists are concerned that genetic engineering brings risks and could do irreversible damage to life. Genetic engineering has the potential to change human nature. Purity of both the mind and body is necessary for spiritual progress. Even efforts to develop new genetic cures for cancer and inherited genetic diseases often involve the cruel treatment of animals.

Another issue is the prohibition of stealing. Isn't the taking of our genes and those of plants, changing them and then selling them, a form of stealing? Buddhists have real concerns about putting human genes into plants or animals. The karma from the harming of life in developing gene therapy or cloning may cause even greater problems in the future.

> ### ❓ Questions
> 1 Briefly explain Buddhist teaching about the cycle of life.
> 2 What do Buddhists say about fertility treatments?
> 3 What are the five skandhas? How are they important in the debate about scientific experiments on embryos?
> 4 Explain Buddhist attitudes towards transplant surgery, blood transfusions, human genetic engineering and cloning.

💬 For discussion

1 Do you think that it is right to put human genes into plants or animals? Give reasons. C2.1a

2 'The world is already overpopulated; there is no need for babies to be conceived in a petrie dish.' Do you agree? Give reasons. C2.1a

Aim
To understand Hindu beliefs concerning:
* fertility treatment and surrogacy
* medical research and practice.

Hinduism does not separate humans from God so completely as the western faiths. Brahman, the Supreme Spirit, is in every living creature and so life is very valuable. Indian yogis and mystics speak of the co-creative process of evolution. God is working His will through humans, including scientists. Two principles apply to Hindu views concerning medical research and medical ethics. The first is **ahimsa** (non-injury). The second is what effect will it have on the quest to achieve **moksha** (spiritual liberation, or freedom).

Fertility treatment and surrogacy

Hindu marriage rituals include the praying for abundant and strong offspring. Each family likes to have at least one son. If the couple cannot conceive without help, medical aid is allowed. Hindus do not usually consider surrogacy, but in the case of infertility, adoption of a son from relatives may occur. Hindus do not object to artificial insemination using the husband's sperm (AIH). The use of a donor's sperm (AID) is unacceptable. AID poses problems for tracing the male ancestry and the child would not know for certain to which caste his or her father belonged.

Embryology, transplant surgery and blood transfusions

The use of embryos for scientific experiments causes problems for Hindus because they believe all life is sacred. An embryo is a life and so Hindus are not in favour of destroying it as part of a scientific experiment.

> *'I look upon all creatures equally; none are less dear to me and none more dear.'*
>
> (Bhagavad Gita 9: 29)

Hindu mythology has stories in which parts of the human body are used for the benefit of other humans. The donating of organs for use in transplant surgery is left up to the individual.

Hinduism does not forbid the use of body organs or blood if it helps to relieve the suffering of others.

Genetic engineering and cloning

Human genetic engineering should only happen under strict conditions. Changes may prove to be difficult to reverse.

Hindus ask the question about human cloning, 'Will it help the soul's evolution towards moksha?' Most say that it will not. Some suggest that cloning might provide a home for an advanced soul, needing to live without emotion or powerful desire. But if a duplicate of your body lived on beyond your death, would you, the soul, be held up in the astral plane, awaiting a new birth indefinitely? Having a part of the body remaining alive could prevent freedom.

If done with good intentions it may bring benefit, but if cloning is done for selfish reasons, greed or power, it may bring severe karmic consequences.

? Questions

1 What are Hindu views concerning medical research?

2 Briefly explain Hindu beliefs concerning children and fertility treatments.

3 Explain Hindu attitudes towards embryology, transplant surgery and blood transfusions.

4 Explain some of the concerns Hindus have about human cloning.

For discussion

1 'Playing around with human genes is extremely dangerous.' Do you agree? Give reasons.

2 'Buying and selling sperm, eggs and even the use of wombs, turns children into mere things; items that can be bought and sold.' Do you agree? Give reasons. Citizenship 1a

Aim

To investigate Sikh beliefs concerning:
- fertility treatment and surrogacy
- medical research and practice.

Sikhs believe that God is the creator of all life. There exists in each person the 'divine spark' (the soul). The soul is part of God and will be re-absorbed into Him after liberation (freedom) takes place from the cycle of birth, death and rebirth (**mukti**). The cycle of rebirths does not allow for human interference.

'By Divine Law are beings created; …
Others by His Law are whistled around in cycles
of births and deaths.'

(Japji 2)

Fertility treatment and surrogacy

Tradition rather than specific Sikh religious teaching demands that the married couple have children. A son is wanted to carry on the family name and to care for the parents in their old age.

If the married couple fail to conceive by natural means, fertility treatments, such as IVF and AIH are permitted. Sikhs believe that procreation (having children) should be between husband and wife, so AID and surrogacy are not allowed.

Embryology, transplant surgery and blood transfusions

To most Sikhs, the embryo is already a person from the moment of conception. The production of embryos for scientific research is not allowed but spare embryos from, for example, IVF treatment may be used. A minority view within Sikhism is that life really begins at 120 days.

Blood transfusions and organ transplants are acceptable within the Sikh religion. The sale of an organ would normally be regarded as unethical and not in keeping with the Sikh tradition, but the donation of an organ from a person who has died, would be regarded as an act of kindness on behalf of the dead person's relatives.

Genetic engineering and cloning

Gene therapy to cure or prevent diseases or defects is not opposed, but the issues concerning cloning are complex. Few would have a problem with cloning fruit or vegetables in order to obtain a certain quality, appearance and flavour, but what about humans and animals? The answer is not given in Sikh sacred writings, for example, Guru Granth, in Sikh history, or in its Reht Maryada (Code of Conduct). The Gurus recognized that time and new technology brings new questions.

Before an action is taken, Sikhs believe they should ask questions, such as, 'Would the Guru approve of what I am about to do? If everyone did what I am about to do, would that be all right?' God has given humans the knowledge of science and a mind to discuss the moral implications. The question has to be asked as to whether cloning will be of benefit to the human race, physically and spiritually. Cloning could be used to provide organs for transplant, but most Sikhs are still uncertain as to the right approach to be given towards the potential scientific developments surrounding this whole issue.

❓ Questions

1 Who do Sikhs believe is responsible for life?

2 Why do Sikh families particularly want a son?

3 Which forms of fertility treatment are allowed and not allowed in Sikhism? Give reasons.

4 Explain the Sikh position concerning the use of embryos, blood transfusions and organ transplants.

5 What questions are important to Sikhs when considering issues, such as genetic engineering and cloning?

💬 For discussion

'There is nothing wrong in selling body parts. More donations will be made and so there will be less shortage of organs.' Do you agree? Give reasons. C2.1a

Aim

To review a summary of the important issues concerning religious attitudes to matters of life and to study some exam questions.

Now that you have considered the difficult religious issues on matters of life, it is time to see if you can answer the type of question that will appear in exams. Before you do so, have a look at the factfile summary to check how much you know.

Factfile summary

I need to make sure that I:

- know and understand the beliefs and teachings concerning when life begins, and the implications of these in relation to developments in medical research for the religion(s) that I have studied. To obtain high marks I will need to use relevant quotes from sacred writings.

- understand technical terms, such as the sanctity of life, sexual intercourse, surrogacy, AIH, AID, IVF (test tube babies), embryology, blood transfusion, transplant surgery, human genetic engineering and cloning.

- am familiar with the law and the contemporary debate concerning issues like surrogacy, scientific research using embryos, and cloning.

- consider the ethical, moral and practical implications of developments in medicine and medical research.

- can explain and evaluate the views of others (including believers), as well as expressing own point of view on the issues concerning matters of life.

Exam questions

1 **a** Explain what is meant by *in vitro* fertilization and why it is used. [5 marks]

   b Explain what is meant by cloning and the relevance of religious beliefs to this issue. [10 marks]

   c 'There is nothing wrong with using human embryos for medical research.' How far do you agree? Give reasons for your answer, showing that you have thought about more than one point of view. Refer to religious teachings in your answer. [5 marks]

2 **a** Explain what is meant by surrogacy. Briefly explain the legal position regarding surrogacy in Britain. [5 marks]

   b Explain religious teachings and beliefs that might influence people when considering the different types of fertility treatment. [10 marks]

   c 'There is no doubt about it; life begins at conception.' How far do you agree? Give reasons for your answer, showing that you have thought about more than one point of view. Refer to religious teachings in your answer. [5 marks]

3 **a** Explain the concerns that religious people might have about human genetic engineering. [5 marks]

   b Explain religious beliefs and attitudes towards transplant surgery and the use of blood transfusions. [10 marks]

   c 'The cloning of humans would be science going one step too far.' How far do you agree? Give reasons for your answer, showing that you have thought about more than one point of view. Refer to religious teachings in your answer. [5 marks]

Care for the sick and the elderly

Aim
To investigate the role of the family and the community in caring for the terminally ill and the elderly.

We live in an ageing population. Modern medical science and better living conditions have combined to allow people to live longer. A hundred years ago only one in 20 people of Britain's population was aged over 65. Now the figure has risen to almost one in five. The number of senior citizens is set to rise further as those born during the 'baby boom' years following World War II reach retirement. Many people who are retired stay healthy and live for many years, but old age may bring financial difficulties, failing health and loneliness. Many elderly people need the support of others. This may come from the family, the state and religious communities.

A birthday party in a senior citizen's home

In previous generations the extended family would have taken care of the elderly. Several generations lived together or close by. In Britain today, often marriage or employment has taken the younger generation to other parts of the country. In other cases, retired people may move away from those they know to live by the coast or in the country.

Nuclear families (the parents plus the children), single-parent families and families where the parents have remarried (reconstituted or step-families) has made the looking after of ageing parents more complicated. If a grandparent dies it is not always easy for the remaining partner to sell the home and leave friends behind in order to be near their children. Similarly, the children may have difficulties in moving as it could mean changing jobs, selling their homes and uprooting from the community in which they are involved.

Community care schemes, including home helps and the meals-on-wheels service, make it possible for most elderly people to stay in their own homes. The time may arrive when this is no longer possible. Failing health may mean that they are unable to look after themselves.

Homes for the elderly

Local authorities provide warden-controlled units where the residents are able to live independently, knowing that help is near by if required – the pressing of an alarm button alerts the warden if a resident needs help. The Social Services Department runs residential homes for those with more serious disabilities. These homes provide communal meals and activities for the residents. Some offer day care or short stays, so that the carers of the elderly are able to have a break.

Nursing homes, run by the health authorities, provide 24-hour-a-day nursing care for those who require it. There are homes for the mentally frail, as well as those who specialize in caring for patients with physical disabilities. Fees for these residential and nursing homes reflect the financial situations of their patients. These homes are expensive to run and places are limited. Private residential and nursing homes are also available for those who can afford their fees.

Hospitals and hospices

Hospitals provide treatment for the elderly with curable illnesses, but patients suffering from a terminal illness are moved to a hospice. This is a home that cares only for the dying. Here the aim of the treatment is to relieve suffering and control their symptoms in the most effective way. This approach is known as palliative care. The emphasis is on quality of life. Patients are encouraged to be as fulfilled as possible physically, mentally and spiritually.

> *'The goal of palliative care is achievement of the best quality of life for patients and their families.'*
>
> (World Health Organization, 1990)

The aim is to relieve anxiety and patients are encouraged to talk about and prepare for death. Their families are also involved in the process and the objective is to allow people to die with dignity. Hospices are available to all, irrespective of religion, but most hospices in Britain are Christian foundations.

There are 2000 Macmillan nurses and 300 Macmillan doctors supporting families in Britain

? Questions

1 Explain the meaning of the terms:
   a extended family
   b nuclear family
   c single-parent family
   d reconstituted or step-families.
2 'It should be the responsibility of the children to look after their ageing parents.' How far do you agree?
3 What is meant by the term 'palliative care'?
4 How does the hospice movement aim to relieve suffering?

For discussion

It is said that elderly people have the choice of what to do if their health begins to fail. Discuss and record what options are available and the advantages and disadvantages of each choice. PS2.1

For research

1 Find out more about the hospice movement. Several Internet sites have relevant information. IT2.1

2 Macmillan Cancer Relief is a UK charity supporting people with cancer and their families with specialist information, treatment and care from the time of diagnosis and throughout their experience of cancer. Find out more about their work by accessing their Internet site. IT2.1

3 From your research, give a short talk to the class about the hospice movement or Macmillan nurses. C2.1b

Death and euthanasia

Aim
To investigate:
- definitions of death
- decision making concerning the use of life-support machines
- the concepts of sanctity and quality of life
- the meaning of the term euthanasia.

When is a person dead?

The usual definition of death states that it is when the heart stops beating and/or the lungs stop working. This is known as cardio-respiratory death. What, however, is the status of someone who is 'brain dead'? Brain death means the irreversible loss of all brain function. A person who is 'brain dead' cannot breathe without the help of a machine.

Comas

Perhaps as the result of a car crash or accident a person may lapse into a coma. This is a sleep-like condition arising from injury to the brain stem. For most patients this is only a temporary condition, but how would you describe the status of someone in a long-term coma? Some patients are in a permanent vegetative state. In this condition the brain stem is still alive and the person still breathes without help. They are, however, completely unaware of themselves and their environment. This is because the cerebral cortex (the thinking, feeling and communicating part of the brain) is totally damaged and cannot be repaired. Is such a person really alive?

It isn't always easy to make the decision about whether or not to continue life by artificial means. Sometimes coma victims may never regain consciousness or they may partially recover but have permanent brain damage. On other occasions, someone may be in a coma for weeks before coming out of it and then, after a rehabilitation programme, make a full recovery. It is often a time of suffering not only for the victims, but also for their loved ones. Some coma victims are kept alive using a life-support machine. Are there occasions when it would be better to switch off these machines?

A mother's dilemma

'My son was knocked down by a hit and run driver. He was found unconscious and he has been in a coma for months. It is so distressing to visit the hospital each day to see no sign of recovery. John is being kept alive by a machine. The doctors can give me no hope.'

The sanctity of life

Some people believe that life is something sacred. They argue that all living things have a right to life. Martin Luther King, the American civil rights leader said:

'We need to affirm the sacredness of all human life. Every person is somebody because he is a child of God.'

All the major religions stress the importance of caring for and respecting the seriously ill. Some people argue, however, that there are times when the quality of life is so poor that it is justifiable to end life to prevent further suffering. None of the main world religions generally support the idea of suicide.

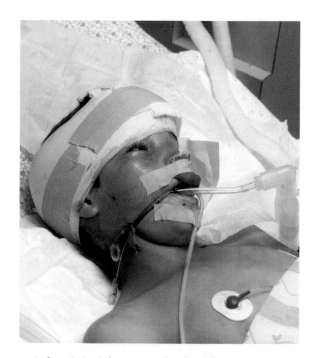

When is it right to switch off a life-support machine?

The Samaritans counsel people who are considering suicide. The group was founded in 1953 by the Revd Chad Varah, rector of St Stephen's Church, in London

Euthanasia

The word euthanasia comes from the Greek words *eu* and *thanatos*. Together these words mean 'a gentle (good) death'. Nowadays, the meaning has been widened to include how that gentle (good) death is brought about. Sometimes it is called **mercy killing**.

There are various forms of euthanasia:

- Voluntary euthanasia – this is helping someone to die when the person has asked to end his or her life in order to avoid further suffering. A typical example would be when a person is suffering from an incurable and painful illness.

- Involuntary (compulsory) euthanasia – this is when someone else makes the decision, for example, a doctor or the state – killing the sick or elderly without their permission or against their will.

- Non-voluntary euthanasia – this is the ending of the life of a patient who is not capable of giving his or her permission. The person who carries out the euthanasia may do so believing that it is in the best interests of the patient.

- 'Passive euthanasia' – this is the taking away or withholding of treatment with the intention of ending life. Examples include withholding or withdrawing life-support machines or not giving life-prolonging drugs. In some instances, patients are given pain-relieving treatment in such high doses that they may die more quickly. This is known as the double effect.

- Active euthanasia – this is when a doctor deliberately intervenes to end life.

- Suicide – this is used to describe the act of killing oneself.

? Questions

1 When do you think a person is dead?
2 Write a letter to John's mother giving her advice on what to do. C2.3
3 Under what circumstances do you think a life-support machine should be switched off? Give reasons.
4 What is meant by the 'sanctity of life' and 'the quality of life'?
5 What is meant by the term euthanasia?
6 Explain the different types of euthanasia.

For discussion

1 Who should make decisions about when to use and when to turn off life-support machines?

2 Is there ever a time when life is worthless and no longer worth living?

For research

There are groups such as the Samaritans who help counsel people who are considering suicide. Find out about the Samaritans organization, for example, use their Internet site. IT2.1

Euthanasia, suicide and the law

Aim
To investigate:
- the legality of suicide and euthanasia
- some of the problems associated with treating terminally ill patients.

Voluntary euthanasia and the law

Voluntary euthanasia is now legal in Switzerland, the US State of Oregon and in the Netherlands, but there are strict conditions.

In the Netherlands, it is only legal if the patient has made a voluntary and informed request or is in unbearable pain and cannot be helped medically. Before the change in the law, voluntary euthanasia was illegal and a crime, but for more than 15 years Dutch doctors were able to carry it out if they followed strict guidelines laid down by the courts and the Royal Dutch Medical Association.

The Dutch Remmelink Report, 1990 revealed the extent to which euthanasia is being used in the Netherlands. Out of the annual death rate of 130 000, it was estimated that:

- 2300 died as the result of doctors granting their patients request by putting them to death (active voluntary euthanasia).

- 400 died as a result of doctors giving patients the means to kill themselves (doctor-assisted suicide).

- 1040 died from involuntary euthanasia. That is an average of almost three people a day put to death by their doctors without their knowledge or consent. Of these, 72 per cent had never said they wanted to end their lives.

- 8100 died as a result of drugs that were given, not primarily to control pain, but to speed up the patient's death.

The main reasons for the decision to end these lives were 'low quality of life', 'the family could not cope anymore' and 'there was no prospect for the patient's improvement'.

In Britain, voluntary euthanasia is illegal, although many people would support a change in the law. Until 1961 it was a criminal offence to take one's own life.

The Hippocratic Oath

To become a doctor it was necessary to take the Hippocratic Oath.

'I will use treatment to help the sick according to my ability and judgement, but never with a view to injury and wrongdoing. Neither will I administer a poison to anybody when asked to do so, nor will I suggest such a course ... But I will keep pure and holy both my life and art.'

(The Hippocratic Oath)

This oath makes it impossible for doctors to practise euthanasia, but the BMA *News Review* in September 1996 showed that the medical profession was divided over euthanasia. Over 750 GPs and hospital doctors were surveyed – 46 per cent said that they supported a change in the law to allow them to carry out euthanasia if the patient requested it; 44 per cent supported the present law; 37 per cent said that they would be prepared to carry out euthanasia if the law allowed it (see chart).

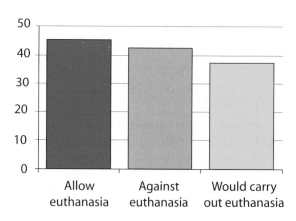

The BMA's 1996 survey of doctors on euthanasia

Euthanasia and the courts

The law courts in some cases grant permission for 'passive euthanasia'. An example of this is when consent is given to turn off the life-support machine when a person is already 'brain dead'.

Sometimes a doctor has to decide whether or not to give drugs which ease pain, but also have the consequence of bringing death nearer. The legality of giving such a 'double or dual effect' drug, that is helpful in one way but also advances death, is not totally clear in British law. Dr Michael Irwin, an American doctor who supports voluntary euthanasia, has said that he estimates that up to 100 000 people in the USA are helped to die through dual effect every year.

In Britain there have been some examples where the courts have examined what the doctors have done:

- In 1957, an Eastbourne GP, Dr John Bodkin Adams, was accused of killing an elderly patient in order to benefit from her will. He argued during his trial that we should do what we can to 'ease the passing'. The jury rejected the police evidence and Dr Adams was acquitted. Much of the media had been convinced that he had been responsible for poisoning many rich old ladies after altering their wills in his favour.

- In 1992, Dr Nigel Cox received a suspended prison sentence for giving an elderly arthritis sufferer a lethal injection of potassium chloride.

- In 1999, Dr David Moor was charged with murder after he had given George Liddell, 85, a lethal dose of diamorphine. He said that all he had done was to try and relieve his patient's agony, his distress and his suffering, but the injection had caused the terminally ill patient to die. The Newcastle GP was acquitted after the judge and jury decided that when the only way to relieve someone's agony is, effectively, to kill them, it is not a criminal but a compassionate act.

- In 1993, the Law Lords made an important decision when they established a right for doctors to withdraw artificial feeding pipes from irreversibly damaged patients. This occurred in the case of Tony Bland, who lay in a coma for months after the tragic events at Hillsborough (Sheffield Wednesday's football ground) in 1989.

'I'm worried that I will suffer great pain.'

Sheila's request

'I am a diabetic and I am going blind. I have arthritis in my hands and chronic narrowing of the arteries, which has already resulted in the amputation of my left leg. I have no family commitments and I am not afraid of dying. But I am afraid of long, drawn out suffering preceding my death in the natural course of events. If the time comes, I would like to be able to say that enough is enough. It would be a great comfort to me to know that there is a doctor to whom I can turn.'

❓ Questions

1 Explain the legal position in Britain concerning euthanasia and suicide.

2 Do you think that if people continue to live longer that the law may be changed in more countries? Give reasons for your opinion.

3 Explain the relevance of the Hippocratic Oath to the euthanasia debate.

4 Read 'Sheila's request'.
   a Explain what she is saying.
   b Do you think she should be allowed to use euthanasia?

💬 For discussion

Should doctors be prosecuted if they give a terminally ill patient a pain-relieving drug that they know will kill the patient?

The euthanasia debate

Aim

To consider:

- the rights of those involved
- the arguments for and against euthanasia.

There are pressure groups, such as the Voluntary Euthanasia Society, who take the view that people should have the right to make their own decision about their own death. They suggest that members make a 'Living Will' to declare that they do not wish their lives to be artificially prolonged in the event of a terminal illness, or if they are in a permanent state of unconsciousness. Some carry a medical emergency card, which states that if there is no reasonable prospect of recovery, then they do not wish to be resuscitated or to have their life prolonged artificially.

MEDICAL EMERGENCY CARD

supplied by

VOLUNTARY EUTHANASIA SOCIETY

13 Prince of Wales Terrace London W8 5PG 020 7937 7770

My Full name is

If there is no reasonable prospect of recovery I do NOT wish to be resuscitated or my life to be artificially prolonged My Advance Directive is lodged with

1. Medical Information eg. blood group

2. After my death my organs may be used for medical purposes

3. Next of Kin

Signature

Date

A medical emergency card

What are the rights of those involved?

In considering the issue of euthanasia what are the rights of those concerned?

- Does a person have the right to die if he or she so wishes? Perhaps the person cannot face any more pain, or feels that his or her useful life is over and wishes to have a dignified end to life. Should the individual have the right to **self-determination** (being able to decide for themselves what happens to them)? Does he or she need protection from making a decision, which once acted upon cannot be reversed?

- It is not easy for relatives and friends to watch a loved one suffering from becoming old and infirm or in agony from an incurable illness. We put animals down if they are suffering, shouldn't relatives have a right to make the same type of decision for an elderly member of their family? Or would it be too tempting to make decisions based on self-interest and greed, for example, what if people knew they would inherit a great deal of wealth once their relative died?

- Doctors often see great suffering that they aren't able to cure. Should doctors have the right to end such suffering by giving the patient one lethal injection?

- Then there are the rights of society as a whole. Keeping alive thousands of very infirm and suffering people costs a lot of money. Is it right to expect society to pay when there is no hope for the elderly recovering and leading a 'useful' life again?

- Is it necessary for the courts to make a decision concerning the rights of individual cases or should the present law remain unchanged?

Some religions teach that God gave us life and, therefore, He alone has the right to decide when life should end.

Whatever the rights of the individual, it is important to realize that the death of a person has an effect on those who are left behind, especially those who grieve for their loved one.

The arguments for euthanasia

- Death with dignity is better than a long lingering painful death.

- At least 5 per cent of terminal pain cannot be fully controlled and other distressing symptoms, such as incontinence or sickness cannot always be relieved.

- Doctors are aware when there is no hope of recovery and when a patient is in great pain.

- An injection can quickly and humanely end the suffering.

- Despite the law, a survey published in 1994 in the *British Medical Journal* showed that some doctors are prepared to help patients to die.

- Shouldn't everyone have the right to a good quality of life and to choose how he or she lives and dies?

- Relations and friends suffer when they see their loved one in pain – death may be a 'happy release'.

- We put down animals rather than let them suffer, so why refuse the same merciful release to human beings?

- With the average age of the population getting steadily older, we may not be able to afford to take care of old and infirm people in the future.

The arguments against euthanasia

- Euthanasia is a form of murder.

- It is 'playing God' to decide that a person's life should end. Who has the right to decide?

- Every person has the right to live.

- The doctors may make an incorrect diagnosis. People have recovered after being 'written off' as incurable.

- Modern pain-killing drugs ensure that no one need suffer to an unbearable degree.

- Old people often feel themselves to be a nuisance to their younger relatives and may feel they owe it to loved ones to accept the offer of euthanasia if it is available.

- Life is a gift from God and is sacred. Euthanasia devalues life by making it disposable.

- It would be wrong to expect doctors to kill their patients. The Hippocratic Oath expressly forbids it.

- If we allow voluntary euthanasia it is only one step away from compulsory euthanasia.

- What is needed is love and care for the elderly and sick, not an instant end to their lives.

❓ Questions

What do you think are the most important arguments for and against euthanasia? Give reasons.

💬 For discussion

1 You have been asked to give a talk on euthanasia in a radio debate. The producer says you can argue for or against it to give a young person's view, but you only have 60 seconds to make your point. What should your speech say? C2.1a

2 Role-play a situation where those taking part argue for their rights. Characters could include a doctor, a relative, a member of the Voluntary Euthanasia Society, an elderly person who wishes to die naturally, a judge and a taxpayer. C2.1a

◆ For research

In Britain today there are pressure groups that oppose and some that support the legalization of voluntary euthanasia. Search for and select relevant information that could be used in a debate about euthanasia by using the Internet. IT2.1

Care for the elderly

Christian teaching stresses the importance of treating the elderly with respect and honour (Exodus 20: 12). Although old age brings its problems, Christians are encouraged to recognize the experience and wisdom associated with age. Senior citizens need love and care whether they are living on their own, in an extended family, or in a residential home.

Many Christian Churches provide visitors, senior citizen groups, homes or sheltered accommodation for members of their denominations. The clergy and lay members of the community often lead services in residential homes and local Christian groups may provide special outings or gift parcels for the elderly. Christians are also involved in providing love and care for the dying and support for their families through the hospice movement (see page 34-5).

Suicide and euthanasia

The Bible includes many references to the value of life and expresses the belief that life is a sacred and precious gift from God (Genesis 1: 27). Christians believe that to take a person's life breaks one of the Ten Commandments, that is, *Do not commit murder* (Exodus 20: 13).

Acts 17: 26 states that God has fixed our life span. God gives life and so he alone has the right to take it away. Suicide is therefore regarded as wrong, but most Christians nowadays recognize that people who attempt to kill themselves need to be treated with gentle and loving care. In the past, some denominations regarded suicide as such a sin that they would not bury suicide victims in consecrated ground. The Society of Friends (Quakers) would bury those who had taken their own life and did not take such a view.

Christians recognize that the euthanasia debate is a complex one. There are a variety of Christian views. Some believe that euthanasia is always wrong. Pope Paul VI summed up the teaching of the Roman Catholic Church when he said:

> *'Without the consent of the person euthanasia is murder. His consent would make it suicide. Morally this is a crime which cannot become legal by any means.'*

Some Christians support the turning off of a life-support system if the patient is 'brain dead'. Others believe that it is extremely important to show compassion to those who are suffering. They interpret *'Love your neighbour as you love yourself'* (Mark 12: 31) as meaning that in extreme cases of suffering no further active treatment to prolong life should be given.

Life after death

> *'For Christians, death is not a disaster, but a new beginning. Therefore, attempts to preserve life at any cost should be questioned. Terminally ill patients need to be able to die in peace among those who love and care for them.'*
>
> (Church of England Board of Social Responsibility)

Christians believe in life after death because of the resurrection (rising from the dead) of Jesus.

> *'Christ has been raised from death, as the guarantee that those who sleep in death will also be raised.'*
>
> (1 Corinthians 15: 20)

Jesus promised that he had gone to prepare a place for believers (John 14: 2–3) so we should not be frightened of death. This belief is a source of comfort for both the dying and their relatives.

Some Christians, for example, the **Calvinists**, believe that we are predestined (it is already decided) to go to heaven or hell. This is the belief that God has decided before we are born whether or not we will enjoy eternal life in heaven. Most Christians, however, believe that we have freedom of choice and it depends on our beliefs and confession as much as on our actions as to whether we go to heaven. They believe that:

'If you confess that Jesus is Lord and believe that God raised him from death, you will be saved.'

(Romans 10: 9)

The **Apostles' Creed** states that there is a Day of Judgement when Jesus *'will come again to judge the living and the dead'* (see Revelation 20: 11–12). The souls of believers will go to heaven and live with God for eternity. Roman Catholics and Orthodox Christians (but not Protestants) usually believe in Purgatory, a place where the soul of the person is purified ready to enter heaven. Hell, a place cut off from the presence of God, awaits the souls of evil doers.

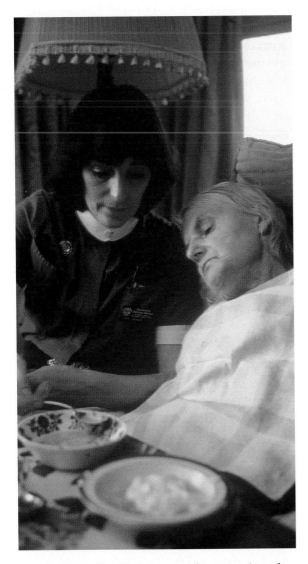

All who work with dying people are anxious that terminal care everywhere should become so good that no one need ever ask for voluntary euthanasia

? Questions

1 Describe how and why Christians try to give practical support to the elderly, terminally ill and their families.

2 Explain the main teachings that guide a Christian when considering the issue of ending a life.

3 Why might a religious believer say that suicide is wrong? Give reasons.

4 The Roman Catholic Church opposes all forms of euthanasia, but some denominations are not totally opposed to 'passive euthanasia'. Explain the different views within the Christian religion.

5 Explain the beliefs about life after death in the Christian religion.

6 'Belief in an after-life is a great comfort to those who are dying.' Do you agree? Give reasons.

For discussion

Does belief in a Day of Judgement and an after-life affect behaviour in this life?

For research

Dame Cecily Saunders is seen as the founder of modern palliative (control of pain) care. Use the Internet to find out and record more about her life and work. IT2.1

Islam

Aim

To understand Muslim teachings and beliefs concerning:

- care for the elderly
- suicide and euthanasia
- life after death.

Care for the elderly

Within the Islamic community you rarely find residential homes for the elderly. Muslims consider it an honour, blessing and opportunity for great spiritual growth to look after and care for parents. In Islam, serving one's parents is a duty second to prayer and it is the right of the elderly to expect it. To send them to a home for the elderly is thought to be unkind and disrespectful.

Suicide and euthanasia

The ideas of the 'right to die with dignity' and 'sparing the patient unbearable pain' are not acceptable to Muslims. Islam teaches that as it is Allah who created life, it is He alone who should decide whether you live or die.

> 'Allah fixes the time span for all things.'
>
> (Surah 53)

To decide when a person should die is to try to 'play God'. Life is a sacred gift from Allah and Allah has decided how long we should live.

> 'When their term expires, they would not be able to delay for a single hour, just as they would not be able to anticipate it.'
>
> (Surah 16: 61)

Suffering is for a purpose, so if a person is in pain, this is not a reason for euthanasia. The Shari'ah includes conditions under which a life may be taken, and mercy killing is not one of them.

Terminating life is forbidden. If a person suffers it is the will of Allah who is testing them. As Allah is compassionate, endurance and patience brings reward.

Muslims do not oppose the turning off of a life-support machine if all hope of recovery has gone.

Life-prolonging drugs need not be given when a person has no chance of awakening out of a coma because to prolong life unnaturally is to go against the purposes of Allah.

The Prophet Muhammad taught that it is wrong to take one's own life. In the **Hadith** it says that killing oneself with either a sword or with poison or by throwing oneself off a mountain will result in torment on the **Day of the Resurrection**.

Life after death

In Islam, the name given for life after death is Akhirah. Muslims believe that the soul is taken to a state of waiting (Barzakh) until the time when Allah will test everyone's characters. This will occur on the Day of Judgement. At this time all will rise from the dead and will have to give an account of their lives. Allah will test each person's reactions to both good fortune and misfortune to see if they are full of complaint or are arrogant or proud or dishonest and unforgiving. Muslims believe that all people earn their own salvation.

The worthy – those who pass Allah's test – will join Allah in Paradise, a place of great delight and reward. Unbelievers and those who are greedy, spiteful and selfish will suffer misery and despair in jahannam (hell), a place of eternal torment.

> 'I warn you of the flaming fire. None shall be cast into it but the most wretched.'
>
> (Surah 92: 14–16)

? Questions

1 In what ways can a Muslim honour the old people in the family?
2 Why do Muslims oppose suicide and voluntary euthanasia?
3 Why might a Muslim support passive euthanasia?
4 Outline the main Muslim beliefs concerning life after death.

For discussion

Why do Muslims believe that it is possible for a compassionate God to allow people to suffer?

Aim

To understand Jewish teachings and beliefs concerning:

- care for the elderly
- suicide and euthanasia
- life after death.

Care for the elderly

Judaism teaches that elderly people should be respected and honoured.

'Show respect for old people and honour them.'

(Leviticus 19: 32)

The family is encouraged to look after the ageing parents, but it is recognized that this is not always possible. Jewish communities have therefore set up homes that provide care for the very elderly and the very frail. In Britain, Jewish Care provides residential, day, home, dementia, nursing and respite care. The organization works with other Jewish care services, such as home care, special day care centres, carers services and residential nursing homes.

Suicide and euthanasia

Judaism teaches that life is a great blessing that is given to us by God (Genesis 1: 27). It is God the creator who decides when we are to be born and when we should die. However desirable it may seem, euthanasia is 'playing God'.

'He sets the time for birth and the time for death.'

(Ecclesiastes 3: 2)

Suicide is regarded as such a serious sin that those who commit it are buried in a separate part of the cemetery. Judaism is opposed to active euthanasia.

'Respect your father and your mother.'

(Exodus 20: 12)

Some Jews see passive euthanasia in a different light.

'If death is certain, and the patient suffers greatly, it is permissible to desist from postponing death by artificial means.'

(*A Guide to Jewish Religious Practice* by Isaac Klein, KTAV, 1979)

Life after death

Jews refer to a cemetery as **Bet Hayyim**, which means 'House of Life'. Judaism teaches that death is not the end, but there are a variety of beliefs about the world to come. The **Talmud** warns against guessing about this world as 'no eye has seen it'. Many Jews believe that life in this world is preparation for the life that occurs after death.

'This world is like a vestibule before the world to come; prepare yourself in the vestibule that you may enter into the hall.'

(Jewish Book of Daily Prayer)

Most Jews believe that there will be a **resurrection** of the dead. They look forward to the coming of the **Messianic Age**. The righteous Jews (those who have served God and behaved morally) will then be brought back and God and his angels will judge the non-Jews. The unrighteous (the wicked and ungodly) will go to gehinnom (hell) for the cleansing of their souls from sins. The cleansing may last for up to a year.

? Questions

1 Why might a Jew say that active euthanasia is like 'playing God'?
2 Explain why some Jews would support passive euthanasia in certain circumstances.

For discussion

How might Jewish children obey the commandment to honour their parents?

For research

Make notes about Jewish Care. Visit their website to get more information.

Aim
To understand Buddhist teachings and beliefs concerning:
- care for the elderly
- suicide and euthanasia
- life after death.

Care for the elderly

Buddhism teaches that it is important to respect the elderly and to concentrate on celebrating the essential goodness and wisdom of the person. Buddhists acknowledge that the courage of the old can help to inspire family, friends and others. Their care organizations offer support for the physical, emotional, intellectual, cultural and spiritual needs of the individual and their families. Help is given to enable people to stay in their homes with their families for as long as possible, but where this is impossible Buddhists work with agencies, such as hospices, which care for the terminally ill.

Suicide and euthanasia

The first of the **Five Precepts** is to keep from harming any living things (**Ahimsa**). Buddhists believe in non-violence and respect for life. Taking life is, therefore, against the first precept. Care and support for the dying is to be encouraged.

Despite the teaching of Ahimsa, decisions about euthanasia may not be easy. **The Eightfold Path** includes **Right Intention** and **Right Action**. What is the reason for recommending euthanasia? Is it to avoid responsibilities towards an elderly person, or is it to show compassion towards someone who is suffering terribly and wishes to die? Each case needs to be considered on its own merits. Whatever is decided should cause the least amount of pain and suffering.

'The purpose of being born as a human being is to eliminate the suffering of others and to bring them happiness.'

(Lama Thubten Zopa Rinpoche)

The action taken will affect **karma**, also know as kamma (actions in the previous life). Suicide, murder or euthanasia for the wrong reason will lead to negative karma and bring about more suffering for all those involved in a future life.

Life after death

Buddhists believe in the idea of 'again becoming' (or rebirth).

'The body dies but the spirit is not entombed.'

(Dhammapada 151)

This does not mean that a soul of a person moves on into another life (the Buddha taught that the soul does not have any real existence), but that a new life will be formed that is affected by the life that is ending. The energy created by the major actions in the previous life of a person sets another life in motion. The process of birth, death and rebirth is called **samsara**. The form of the return, or rebirth, depends on karma. Being reborn in a 'better' birth is seen as a stepping stone towards entering Nibbana. Nibbana is an eternal state beyond suffering and **impermanence** (constant change).

? Questions

1. Describe how and why Buddhists try to give support to the elderly, terminally ill and their families.
2. Explain the main principles that guide a Buddhist when considering the issues of euthanasia and suicide.
3. Why would a Buddhist say that putting an end to life does not necessarily stop suffering?
4. Why might Buddhists say that each case should be examined on its own merits?
5. Explain the Buddhist beliefs about life after death.

For discussion
What contribution could elderly people make to family life?

Aim
To understand Hindu teachings and beliefs concerning:
* care for the elderly
* suicide and euthanasia
* life after death.

Care for the elderly
Hinduism teaches that old age is to be respected.

> 'Let your mother be a god to you. Let your father be a god to you ...'

(Taittiriya Upanishad 1.11.2)

Suicide and euthanasia
This respect for the elderly and all forms of life means that the elderly, weak, and those who are terminally ill, should be cared for until the right time (kala) has arrived for them to die naturally.

Hindus believe that helping a person to take his or her own life is both a crime and a sin. Hinduism stresses the need to perform their **dharma** (their duty), for example, providing care for the terminally ill. To help someone else to die would attract bad karma and suffering in future rebirths. To prevent this, the motive for euthanasia would have to be totally selfless.

Hinduism does not generally support suicide.

> 'The one who tries to escape from the trials of life by committing suicide will suffer even more in the next life.'

(Yajur Veda 40–3)

In Hindu society, elderly people enjoy great honour from their families

In some situations suicide used to be seen as a religious act of merit. For example, until it was banned, some faithful wives burnt themselves on their husbands' funeral pyres and some Hindus fasted themselves to death.

Life after death
Hindus believe that it is only the body that dies, not the soul (Atman). The soul lives forever and continues in its journey to eventual release from being born again. The circle of birth, death and rebirth is known as samsara. The soul assumes a new body in order to experience the fruits of its good and bad actions in the previous life. The idea of what people sow, they will reap is known as the law of karma.

The ultimate goal is to be near or united with Brahman (the Supreme Spirit, God). When the soul is free from the bondage of the cycle of samsara, it enjoys eternal divine bliss. This release from samsara and the chain of suffering is called **Moksha**.

? Questions
1 How do Hindus believe that they should treat the elderly?
2 What do you think Hindus mean when they say that helping someone to take their life is both a crime and a sin?
3 What effect might helping someone to die have on future rebirths?
4 What is the attitude of Hindus towards suicide?
5 Explain the Hindu beliefs about life after death.

For discussion
'Let your mother be a god to you. Let your father be a god to you ...' How would a Hindu family put this into practice?

Sikhism

Aim

To understand Sikh teachings and beliefs concerning:

- care for the elderly
- suicide and euthanasia
- life after death.

Care for the elderly

Respect for elders is a key principle of Sikh society. It has always been accepted as the duty of sons to care for their parents. The initial reaction towards homes for the elderly by Sikhs from Asia who settled in the west was one of shock and horror. Attitudes have begun to change, but the home and the help of those who meet in the local **gurdwara** are seen as the primary support for the elderly.

Suicide and euthanasia

Most Sikhs oppose euthanasia and suicide, as it is God who gives and takes life.

> *'God sends us and we take birth. God calls us back and we die.'*
>
> (Guru Granth Sahib 1239)

Suffering is part of human life and has a place in God's scheme. Sikhs pray for the grace, strength and courage to endure and accept pain. Some Sikhs believe that they should accept what God gives as an expression of the divine will and that this will should not be interfered with. In other words, nature should take its course. Other Sikhs regard the quality of life as being the most important factor. If a person is in a permanent vegetative state (see page 36), then to stop giving life-prolonging drugs might be acceptable.

Some Sikhs might be sympathetic towards a very weak elderly person who requests death because of the heavy burden he or she is placing on the family. In such a situation, medical and legal safeguards would need to be in place.

Life after death

Sikhs believe in the **rebirth** or **reincarnation** of the soul according to karma (the good or bad actions in the previous life). At death, the soul is reincarnated (reborn) in another body. The exact form depends on how the person's last life has been lived. The soul has existed since creation and evolves or develops from lower life forms.

> *'For several births I was a worm … an elephant, a fish, a deer … a bird, a serpent … a bull, a horse. After a long period has the human frame come into being. Seek now union with the Lord of the Universe, for now is the time.'*
>
> (Guru Granth Sahib 176)

Death brings another step towards ultimate unity with God. The aim is to break free from the cycle of death and rebirth and achieve **mukti** or liberation (freedom). Sikhs believe the way to achieve liberation involves listening to the words of the Gurus, meditating on the Name of God and offering worship in the presence of the Sangat (the congregation of Sikhs).

❓ Questions

1 How do Sikhs view suffering?
2 Are there any circumstances where euthanasia might be acceptable to Sikhs?
3 'Claims that the quality of life is so very poor that the life might as well be ended could be the start on a slippery slope.' Do you agree?
4 Explain the Sikh beliefs about life after death.
5 'Belief in an after-life is a great comfort to those who are dying.' Do you agree? Give reasons.

💬 For discussion

Is it better for the family to look after their elderly parents or to put them in a residential home? Discuss different circumstances.

Aim

To review a summary of the important issues concerning religious attitudes to matters of death and to study some exam questions.

Now that you have considered the difficult religious issues on matters of death, it is time to see if you can answer the type of question that will appear in exams. Before you do so, have a look at the factfile summary to check how much you know.

Factfile summary

I need to make sure that I:

- know and understand the beliefs and teachings concerning life, death and what happens after death for the religion(s) that I have studied. To obtain high marks I will need to use relevant quotes from the sacred writings and/or modern statements from religious leaders.
- understand the role of the family and community in caring for the terminally ill and elderly. This includes the work of homes for the elderly, hospitals and hospices. I need to understand the religious teachings concerning the elderly for the religious traditions I have studied.
- appreciate the problems associated with decision making concerning the use of life-support machines.
- am aware of the problems associated with defining when a person is dead and the issues of sanctity and quality of life.
- am familiar with the current law and the rights of the individual, the family, doctors and others in relation to euthanasia and suicide.
- am able to distinguish between the types of euthanasia, such as voluntary, involuntary, 'passive' and active and the debate about whether euthanasia should be legalized.
- am able to explain and evaluate the views of others (including believers), as well as expressing my own point of view on the issues concerning matters of death.

Exam questions

1 **a** Explain the work of a hospice.   [5 marks]

b How might religious teachings and beliefs influence a person's decision about euthanasia?   [10 marks]

c 'People have the right to decide for themselves whether they should live or die.' How far do you agree? Give reasons for your answer, showing that you have thought about more than one point of view. Refer to religious teachings in your answer. [5 marks]

2 **a** Believers often talk about:

  i the sanctity of life

  ii the quality of life.

  What do they mean by this?   [5 marks]

b Explain the teachings of the two religious traditions you have studied, which may bring comfort to the dying and their loved ones.   [10 marks]

c 'If it is the duty of parents to look after their young children, it is also the duty of children to look after their elderly parents.' How far do you agree? Give reasons for your answer, showing that you have thought about more than one point of view. Refer to religious teachings in your answer.   [5 marks]

3 **a** Explain the meaning of the following terms and explain what the law in Britain says about them:

  i voluntary euthanasia

  ii involuntary euthanasia.   [5 marks]

b How might religious people respond to the viewpoint of a sick person who says, 'I'm dying anyway! Why can't I die NOW?'   [10 marks]

c 'Religion should be there to comfort the dying, but let the doctors make the decisions!' How far do you agree with this comment? Give reasons to support your answer and show that you have thought about different points of view.   [5 marks]

Drugs

> **Aim**
> To investigate:
> - non-medical drugs
> - why people take drugs
> - social and recreational drugs
> - the use of performance enhancing drugs.

What is a drug?

Drugs alter the way the body works and may change the way we feel. For example, some drugs are depressants, some stimulants and others hallucinogens.

Put simply, depressants slow down the central nervous system, while stimulants speed it up. Hallucinogens affect our senses and alter the way we perceive or see things.

Social and recreational drugs

Social drugs are taken to be sociable and to be regarded as part of the group. For example, having a drink at the pub with friends, or smoking with them after a meal. These drugs may help to relax people and so those taking them may become more outgoing and friendly. For those who are old enough, smoking tobacco and drinking alcohol are not illegal. However, some social drugs are not legal, for example, the taking of ecstasy at a rave.

Drugs used by people as part of leisure or relaxation time are known as recreational drugs. It includes legal drugs such as caffeine, alcohol and tobacco. Illegal drugs, such as amphetamines, cocaine, Ecstasy, heroin, ketamine, LSD, marijuana and magic mushrooms are also recreational drugs.

Performance enhancing drugs

In sport, some people wish to gain an advantage over their competitors and, if they think that they can get away with it, are prepared to take drugs to improve their performance. For example, Ben Johnson tested positive having taken a banned substance. He wanted to gain an advantage over his competitors in the 100 metres sprint.

Drugs in sport

The international governing bodies want to stop the use of drugs in their sports. Not only is it cheating and unfair on the others taking part, but many of the substances that are used have harmful side effects. In athletics, for example, after a race the first three and a random selection of other runners may be tested. Competitors have to provide a urine sample. This is taken under strict supervision. If it is proved that banned drugs have been used, the governing body will decide what the punishment should be. This could be a short ban or even a lifetime suspension.

According to *Dagens Nyheter*, a Swedish newspaper, the most drug cheats discovered in 1997 were in the sports of bobsleigh, weightlifting and baseball.

Ben Johnson was stripped of his world title when he tested positive for banned substances

Drug	Effects	Test
Erythropietin (EPO)	Increases stamina by boosting oxygen – carrying red blood cells. Used by cyclists and marathon runners.	Combined blood and urine tests – used for the first time on cyclists at the 2000 Olympics.
Human Growth Hormone (HGH)	Reduces fat and builds lean muscle. Would give an advantage to sprinters, swimmers and rowers.	Not available.
Insulin	Increases strength and power. Could be obtained from diabetics selling their prescriptions.	Not available.
Insulin Growth Factor-1 (IGF-1)	Produces bigger and stronger muscles. Similar to HGH.	Not available.
Oxyglobin	Helps the body obtain and use more oxygen in the blood. Gives an advantage in endurance events.	Not detectable.
Steroids	Helps to build muscle bulk quickly – useful in physical sports such as rugby.	Detectable.
Stimulants	Reduces tiredness and fatigue, increases mental sharpness. Useful in sprinting.	Detectable.

Some of the drugs used by sports cheats

The report stated that there were 69 404 tests and 1090 proved positive. Bobsleigh had 3.27 per cent positive tests, weightlifting 3.16 per cent and baseball 2.85 per cent. The average was 1.57 per cent. Football had the lowest number, with only 0.61 per cent testing positive. In athletics it was 1.29 per cent.

One problem is that some athletes are sometimes found guilty of taking drugs when they did not try to cheat. High-profile British athletes, such as Linford Christie, Dougie Walker and Mark Richardson, tested positive for Nandrolene. All three protested their innocence. Some believe that legal dietary supplements are to blame. UK Athletics has acknowledged that Nandrolene can be 'innocently' consumed and produced.

Another problem is that not all drugs are detectable and cheating does take place. Dozens of athletes withdrew from the 2000 Olympic Games in Sydney when it was announced that blood tests for EPO would be introduced. It is claimed that thousands of athletes use HGH to improve their performance. This is a banned but undetectable substance. It is very difficult to catch those who

are cheating and taking performance enhancing drugs. There are those who are making a lot of money out of providing performance enhancing drugs. They are actively trying to keep one step ahead of the international governing bodies test.

Drug cheats involve criminal gangs, corrupt employees in drugs companies, coaches and officials who wish to see their athlete win, and some doctors and pharmacists.

❓ Questions

1 Explain what the terms depressants, stimulants and hallucinogens mean.
2 Is using performance enhancing drugs cheating?
3 Why do sports cheats sometimes get away with it?

💬 For discussion

'Sports cheats should be banned for life. You will always suspect them if they return to their sport.' Do you agree? Give reasons. Citizenship 2b

Legal drugs

Aim
To investigate the use of:
- caffeine
- tobacco
- alcohol.

Caffeine

Most people have at least one daily dose of caffeine. It occurs naturally in coffee and tea and is added to most soft drinks. Tea leaves and coffee beans contain up to 4 per cent caffeine. Cola-flavoured drinks contain large amounts of this drug. Chocolate, some pain relievers and many energy aids all contain caffeine.

Caffeine is an addictive drug that stimulates the central nervous system and makes a person feel more energetic. Many of the other effects are not so welcome. It increases the blood flow through the kidneys, which produces more urine. Large doses (over 1000 mg) increase the risk of heart attacks, can cause restlessness, sleeplessness, nervousness, excitement, flushed face, palpitations, diarrhoea and rambling flow of thought and speech. The amount of caffeine in a cup of coffee or tea can vary greatly, for example, coffee may contain 30–200 mg. Many middle-aged men tend to be heavy coffee drinkers (that is, have more than five cups a day). Decaffeinated coffee has only 2–4 mg per cup. Whilst overdosing on caffeine will probably be very unpleasant, it is unlikely to kill or cause permanent damage.

Tobacco

Native American tribes were the first to begin smoking around 100 BCE. Europeans first came into contact with tobacco when Christopher Columbus discovered America in 1492. Today there are about 1.1 billion smokers in the world, which is about 17 per cent of the total population. About 6000 billion cigarettes are smoked each year.

Until the link with lung cancer was established in the 1950s, smoking was considered fashionable. It was also very profitable for the government.

It is estimated that £7.4 billion tax will be paid on cigarettes in the UK during 2000–1 – that's 2 per cent of the government's total revenue.

Problems

We now know that smoking is highly dangerous.

- There are over 4000 harmful chemicals in tobacco smoke that affect both the smoker and the passive smoker (those who inhale the smoke in the atmosphere from other people's cigarettes). These include aluminium, copper, lead, mercury and zinc, as well as ammonia, carbon dioxide, carbon monoxide and nicotine.

- It is estimated that smoking causes 80 per cent of lung cancer deaths, around 80 per cent of those die from bronchitis and emphysema, and 17 per cent of all deaths from heart disease. Every year smoking-related illnesses cost the National Health Service (NHS) more than £400 million.

- More than 17 000 children aged less than five are admitted to hospital each year because of the effects of passive smoking.

- This year, 3 million deaths will occur because of smoking. Around 120 000 people die each year in the UK because of tobacco, which is about 330 every day. That is the equivalent of a jumbo jet crashing each day and none of the passengers survivng.

Alcohol

Alcohol is a depressant drug that relaxes the drinker. About nine out of ten adults in Britain drink alcohol. It is estimated that £6.6 billion tax will be paid on alcohol during 2000–1 – that's 1.8 per cent of the government's total revenue.

The average amount drunk per week by men is equivalent to eight pints of beer and for women, three pints of beer. Like tobacco, alcohol causes great problems. Drinking too much causes severe damage to the liver and the brain.

- Alcohol abuse costs industry £2 billion per year as workers stay at home to recover from hangovers and 8–14 million days are lost each year because of excessive drinking.

- It costs the NHS around £150 million to deal with alcohol-related health problems. One in four men admitted to hospital are there because of alcohol abuse and over £50 million is spent by the government as the result of alcohol-related crime.

- 3000 people die each year from drinking too much, but the death toll relating to alcohol is estimated at 28 000 a year. This includes suicides, accidents and diseases like strokes and cancers to which alcohol abuse contributes. 65 per cent of suicide attempts are the result of excessive drinking and one in seven road deaths are the result of drink driving. Around 60 000 people are found guilty or cautioned for drunkenness each year. Young people aged 19–20 are the worst offenders.

Alcoholism

People who are addicted to alcohol are called alcoholics. Alcoholics feel a compulsion to drink despite the problems that it causes them. The symptoms of this disease are:

- an inability to limit the amount drunk on any one occasion

- withdrawal symptoms if drinking is stopped, such as sweating, feeling sick, shaking and anxiety

- the need for more and more alcohol to feel its effects (increased tolerance).

Drinking and driving

Alcohol creates a sense of overconfidence. This is dangerous if people are drinking and driving, as they are prepared to take risks. After drinking the brain works less efficiently, for example, reaction time is slowed down and vision is blurred. Around one in five road deaths are alcohol-related. The legal blood alcohol limit for driving is 80 mg of alcohol in 100 ml of blood. Most offenders are men.

Alcoholics Anonymous

A group of recovered alcoholics set up an organisation called Alcoholics Anonymous to help others to recover from alcoholism and to give support to those with alcohol problems.

? Questions

1 Explain the effects of caffeine.
2 Thousands of people die from smoking each year. So why do people do it?
3 Explain the damage caused by alcohol abuse to the individual and the cost to employers and the country.

For discussion

The government raises a huge amount of tax on tobacco products and alcohol. Is this right? Give reasons for your opinion. C2.1a; Citizenship 2b

For research

Find out more about Alcoholics Anonymous by visiting their website or Quit, an organization for those who wish to stop smoking. Make notes on your findings. IT2.1

Illegal drugs 1

Aim

To investigate:

- why people take illegal drugs
- the law and illegal drugs
- arguments for and against legalizing cannabis.

The illegal drugs trade is an international multi-billion-pound industry. People have taken illegal drugs for centuries, but nowadays they have become much more widely available. Research suggests that more people are taking banned drugs than ever before. Young people in Britain are reported to be taking up to five times more than the average for the rest of Europe.

Why do people take illegal drugs?

- For an escape. Drugs help some people escape from the real world and forget their problems.

- To feel good. Some people take drugs for the pleasure that they feel. When the feeling goes they take more drugs to try and recapture it.

- It is part of the dance and youth culture. Research suggests that many who go clubbing or to 'raves' take drugs like Ecstasy.

- Peer or family pressure. Friends experimenting with drugs pressurize group members to join them.

- As a sign of asserting their independence. Young people may assert their independence by making their own choices.

- They are addicted. Once started, they cannot stop. This may be physical or psychological addiction.

The law and illegal drugs

There are three main laws that deal with drug abuse:

Misuse of Drugs Act, 1971

This Act classified illegal drugs according to how dangerous they are. Class A drugs are the most dangerous, then Class B, and the less dangerous are Class C drugs.

Drug Trafficking Offences Act, 1986

This allowed drug traffickers to be imprisoned and their property confiscated.

Intoxicating Substances (Supply) Act, 1985

This Act made it illegal to sell anyone under the age of 18 a substance that he or she believes is being purchased for the purpose of inhaling the fumes to cause intoxication. Since 1999 it has also been an offence for a retailer to supply gas lighter refills to under-18s. The maximum penalty for breaking this law is a fine of £5000, or up to six months in prison, or both.

Class A drugs	Class B drugs	Class C drugs
Includes cocaine, crack cocaine, Ecstasy, heroin	Includes amphetamines, cannabis/marijuana	Includes anabolic steroids
Maximum penalty: • for possession – 7 years' imprisonment, or a fine, or both. • for supplying – life imprisonment, or a fine, or both.	Maximum penalty: • for possession – 5 years' imprisonment, or a fine, or both. • for supplying – 14 years' imprisonment, or a fine, or both.	Maximum penalty: • for possession – 2 years' imprisonment, or a fine, or both. • for supplying – 5 years' imprisonment, or a fine, or both.

Classification of illegal drugs and legal penalties

'Soft' drugs

Physically non-addictive drugs are often referred to as 'soft' drugs. Usually, people are referring to cannabis. So-called 'soft' drugs are illegal, but are seen as being less dangerous than hard drugs. They are usually more readily available than hard drugs. To begin with some of these drugs may be used to give feelings of pleasure. They may be habit forming and the user may become psychologically dependent on them. With some drugs, tolerance develops, so larger doses are needed to get the required effect. Some believe that Ecstasy ought to be classified as a 'soft' drug, but it has caused several deaths and so is a Class A drug. Many believe that there is a real danger that users will move from soft to hard drugs.

Should cannabis be legalized?

Many believe that smoking cannabis should not be against the law. Here are the views of two teenagers:

Damien: Why are the police wasting so much time searching people for cannabis?

Sadie: It's part of their job, stopping the use of illegal drugs.

Damien: I could understand it if they were looking for heroin, but cannabis is no more dangerous to health than cigarettes. Why should one be legal and the other not?

Sadie: Both cigarettes and cannabis damage health. It could be argued that both should be made illegal.

Damien: I disagree, surely you know that cannabis is very helpful for those who suffer from multiple sclerosis.

Sadie: Scientists are still doing research into that. Cannabis may be OK as a medicine, but it should not be legal for everyone.

Damien: But cannabis is not as addictive as many other illegal drugs. Besides, it makes me feel good and calm, unlike alcohol, which makes people aggressive.

Sadie: That may be true, but many believe that cannabis is a 'gateway' drug. It leads on to more dangerous drugs, such as heroin.

Damien: I don't agree, and anyway, it will stop illegal drug dealers and criminal gangs making a lot of money out of cannabis.

Sadie: If they don't make it out of cannabis, then they will push hard drugs even more.

? Questions

1 Explain how illegal drugs are classified. Give examples of each type and the maximum penalty for possession and supplying. Citizenship 1a
2 What does the term 'soft' drug mean?
3 Describe some of the risks involved in smoking cannabis.

For discussion

Organize a debate to discuss legalizing cannabis. Citizenship 2c; WO2.1

For research

Find out some more facts about drugs and write a short play about a supplier trying to sell cannabis at a nightclub. Citizenship 2a

Drug	Effects	Risks
Cannabis/ marijuana (dope, ganja, grass, hash, pot, weed)	Feelings of euphoria (being on a high), which lasts 2–4 hours, talkativeness, laughter. Increased heart rate. Loss of short-term memory. Confusion. Lack of co-ordination.	No records of fatal overdose but may lead to a coma. Psychological dependence. Similar to those suffered by smokers.
Class B	Decreased social inhibitions (acting without embarrassment). User appears listless. Sleepiness, poor performance at school or work.	Increased risk of infertility.

The effects and risks of taking 'soft' drugs

Aim

To investigate:

- how illegal drugs are taken
- what is meant by 'hard' drugs
- the physical and mental effects of drugs and the risks involved
- the debate on legalizing drugs.

How are illegal drugs taken?

By injection

This is the fastest, most efficient and potentially most dangerous way to take drugs. There are three ways to inject:

- into the muscle
- under the skin (known as skin popping)
- into a vein (mainlining). Mainlining is very dangerous as there is no way of regulating (controlling) the dose. Overdoses can lead to death.

By smoking

With smoking the drug is burnt. The smoke is inhaled into the lungs where it is absorbed into the bloodstream. It is less dangerous than injection as the user is able to regulate the dose more easily.

By inhaling

Some drugs can be sniffed up the nose (for example, cocaine), or inhaled through the mouth.

Drug	Effects	Risks
Cocaine (Coke) Class A	Mental – exhilaration followed by tiredness and depression, hallucinations Physical – increases heart rate, blood pressure, body temperature. Afterwards feel restless, depressed, confused and paranoid	Addiction Death from heart attacks, strokes or respiratory failure Sudden death on first use Risk from shared needles of AIDs or hepatitis
Heroin (Skag, smack) Class A	Mental – users get a 'rush' or 'buzz'. Creates a 'high' – feeling of contentment Physical – first-time use causes vomiting and headaches. Loss of appetite, constipation	Addiction Injection carries risk of infection, for example, HIV Overdosing, unexplained deaths Mental health problems
Ecstasy (Barney Rubble, E, Dove, XTC) Class A	Mental – mild euphoric 'rush' followed by calm. Greater awareness of surroundings, colours and sound. More talkative Physical – stimulates and increases brain activity. Large doses can lead to anxiety, panic and confusion	Flashbacks Overheating and dehydration which can be fatal Linked to liver and kidney problems Damages brain cells
LSD (Acid) Class A	Mental – hallucinations, intensified colours, distorted images. May be left feeling disorientated, anxious and depressed Physical – increased heart rate and blood pressure. Sleeplessness, disorientated	Risk of having a 'bad trip' Convulsions, coma, heart and lung failure Psychological dependence Flashbacks
Solvents glues, gases, aerosols	Mental – hallucinations Physical – tiredness and lack of concentration, headaches, violent behaviour	Nausea, vomiting, blackouts Damage to eye, inner ear, muscles, liver, kidney, lungs, bone marrow, brain and reproductive system

The effects and risks of taking 'hard' drugs

By swallowing or chewing

Drugs may be taken as a pill, a tab (a piece of paper with the drug soaked in it), or chewed. Some are swallowed in liquid powder (dabbed) or wrapped in paper (bombed).

'Hard' drugs

'Hard' drugs are illegal addictive drugs that are classified as Class A and are extremely dangerous. The body begins to rely on these drugs and, after a while, it cannot work normally without them. This is known as physical dependence and if the drug is stopped, then craving takes place. Once addicted, a user will do virtually anything to get enough money to obtain a supply, for example, shop lifting, burglary or prostitution. Drugs in this category include cocaine, crack and heroin.

To stop using these drugs is extremely difficult, as the addict has to go through 'cold turkey' (experience painful withdrawal symptoms). This includes severe anxiety, restlessness, agitation and shaking, headaches, nausea and confusion.

The arguments for legalizing drugs

- Legalizing drugs will stop the drug traffickers making massive profits.

- Drug enforcement costs millions of pounds.

- Drugs will be less appealing because they will not be 'forbidden fruit'.

- Society is losing the war on drugs, so they might as well be legal and have some form of control over it.

- Some legal drugs, like cannabis, are less harmful than smoking or alcohol.

- The individual should be given the choice of whether to take drugs or not.

The arguments against legalizing drugs

- Addicts would still use theft, prostitution or other criminal activities to support their habits.

- If drugs were more easily obtained, even more people would become addicts.

- Drug enforcement costs would drop, but costs from crime, hospital treatment and so on would greatly increase.

- Legalizing drugs would send the wrong message to society. People may start with soft drugs and then move on to hard drugs.

- It is the duty of the government to stop people harming themselves and others.

❓ Questions

1. Explain five reasons why some people take illegal drugs.

2. Describe the methods that can be used to take drugs.

3. What does the term 'hard' drugs mean?

4. Why are hard drugs so dangerous?

5. Explain what is meant by 'cold turkey'.

6. Draw up two columns. In column one put the arguments for legalizing drugs and in column two write the arguments against.

7. 'Legalizing drugs would give people the green light to become users.' Do you agree? Give reasons.

💬 For discussion

Why do people take drugs when they know that they are harmful? Make notes on the key points of the discussion. C2.1a; Citizenship 3a

◆ For research

1. Look for some discussion about drug abuse in a current TV soap, newspaper or a young people's magazine. Share the situation with the class and discuss possible outcomes. C2.1a

2. In groups, find out more about the effects of drugs and organize an awareness campaign. You will need to decide what you are going to do and give tasks to different people. PS2.2; WO2.2

Christianity

Most Christians support the use of drugs if they help a person overcome an illness, but they are opposed to drug abuse.

Smoking

Some Christians do smoke, but it is not something that is encouraged. A healthy lifestyle is much preferred and the dangers of passive smoking are also recognized. Most Christians avoid smoking or seek help to try and give up. There isn't any direct teaching on the subject in the Bible, but Christians are taught to be faithful stewards (Matthew 25: 14–30) and help those who are in need. To most Christians smoking is a waste of money, not pleasant for non-smokers and a health hazard. It is recognized that some people are addicted to nicotine and find it very difficult to stop smoking.

Alcohol

Some Christians are tee-totallers. They have made the decision not to drink alcohol at all.

In the nineteenth century Christians supported organizations like the Band of Hope, which encouraged men not to waste their money on getting drunk while their families did not have enough food and clothing. The Salvation Army has had a policy of abstinence (not drinking alcohol) for over 100 years, particularly as they do a lot of work with alcoholics and drug addicts.

Recognizing that some people find it difficult not to drink too much, some Christians believe that it is better to remove temptation by setting an example of not drinking at all.

Paul wrote to the Church at Rome that:

> *'The right thing to do is to keep from eating meat, drinking wine, or doing anything else that will make your brother or sister fall.'*
>
> (Romans 14: 21)

Many other Christians believe in moderate drinking. They are careful not to drink too much and avoid getting drunk. It is recognized that excessive drinking causes people to do things which they otherwise would not do.

> *'Drinking too much makes you loud and foolish. It's stupid to get drunk.'*
>
> (Proverbs 20: 1)

> *'Do not get drunk with wine, which will only ruin you.'*
>
> (Ephesians 5: 18)

But they see nothing wrong in drinking some alcohol. Jesus drank wine, and at the wedding in Cana he turned water into wine. At the Last Supper Jesus told his followers to share bread and wine as they remember him, and Paul encouraged Timothy to take some wine for medical reasons.

> *'Do not drink water only, but take a little wine to help your digestion, since you are ill so often.'*
>
> (1 Timothy 5: 23)

Illegal drugs

Christians are very concerned about the increased use of illegal drugs. They believe that they should glorify God in their bodies and drug abuse certainly does not do that.

'Surely you know that you are God's temple and that God's Spirit lives in you!'

(1 Corinthians 3: 16)

People whose lives are centred around their drug habit are not bringing glory to God, whether they are addicted to alcohol, cocaine, heroin, or using drugs to cheat in sport.

Those who have had their lives ruined by drugs are viewed as needing help. The Christian reaction is to offer love and compassion. Christian groups, like the Salvation Army, offer a bed for the night and food to those who are living on the streets and may be drinking methylated spirits or taking other drugs. A Christian response is not to stand by and ignore the problem but to help. Jesus taught in the Parable of the Sheep and Goats (Matthew 25: 31–46) and the Parable of the Good Samaritan (Luke 10: 25–37) that his followers have a duty to take practical action to assist. Christians believe in the sanctity of life, that every person is valuable to God and that Jesus died to save all people, however bad they might be.

'Don't you know that your body is the temple of the Holy Spirit, who lives in you and who was given to you by God? You do not belong to yourselves but to God; he bought you for a price. So use your bodies for God's glory.'

(1 Corinthians 6: 19–20)

Some Christians believe it their duty to help rehabilitate drug abusers. For example, Jackie Pullinger left Britain while in her 20s and has spent over 30 years helping the heroin addicts of Kowloon's Walled City, in Hong Kong. Others have set up areas of retreat to help people get off alcohol or addictive drugs. Christians believe that much of the drug abuse is caused by people having empty lives and they argue that taking drugs is a not a good alternative for enjoying the spiritual dimension in life.

The Ethiopian Zion Coptic Church and the Rastafarians from Jamaica are the exceptions in Christianity. They believe that the Bible gives them permission to use marijuana (ganja). They base this on the passages in Genesis that state that God created plants and herbs for the use of humans, for example, Genesis 1: 12 and 29. They claim that marijuana produces a religious experience of a mystical nature, and they smoke, drink and even eat it. Mainstream Christians are totally opposed to using marijuana or any other hallucinatory drug.

Questions

1 Why are members of the Salvation Army encouraged not to drink alcohol?

2 What does it mean to drink in moderation? What events in the Bible are used to support this view?

3 Explain why most Christians are opposed to the use of any illegal drugs.

4 Who has a different view concerning the use of marijuana?

5 Why do many Christians try to help those who have a drug problem? Give examples.

For discussion

'The idea of not drinking, smoking or taking soft drugs does not fit in with living in the twenty-first century.' Do you agree? Give reasons. C2.1a

For research

View the Salvation Army website on alcohol on the Internet. Make notes on the work that it does to help those who have an alcohol problem. IT2.1

Muslims believe that they do not own their bodies but Allah does. It is haram (forbidden) to take anything that is harmful. When considering an issue like drug abuse, Muslims consider whether or not it will cause harm to themselves or others.

Smoking

During the fasting of Ramadan, Muslims are not allowed to smoke, but there isn't a verse in the Qur'an that actually says that smoking is forbidden. Smokers are encouraged to give up because it is addictive and is a danger to health. In the Qur'an, Allah says, '... *do not with your own hands contribute to your destruction*' (Qur'an 2: 195). Muhammad said, '*Anyone who believes in Allah and the Last Day should not hurt his neighbour.*' This is interpreted by Muslims who oppose smoking as warning the smoker that Allah will judge them on any damage they have caused others as a result of their smoke. Passive smoking can cause lung cancer, bronchitis, aggravate asthma, and so on, and can be a real danger to young children. The smell of cigarettes is considered to be unpleasant and unacceptable. It is wrong for a Muslim to smoke in the presence of non-smokers or in a public place.

Alcohol

When Islam first started alcohol was fairly widely drunk. Alcohol may be beneficial when used as a medicine, but Muslims believe that the harm it causes is far greater than any good that comes out of it.

> '*They ask you about drinking and gambling. Say: "There is great harm in both, although they have some benefit for men; but their harm is far greater than their benefit."*'

(Qur'an 2: 219)

Over time, more and more restrictions on drinking alcohol were introduced until finally its use for social drinking was banned altogether.

> '*Believers, wine and games of chance, idols and divining arrows, are abominations devised by Satan. Avoid them, so that you may prosper.*'

(Qur'an 5: 90)

Illegal drugs

The word used by Muslims for an intoxicant (a substance that makes you lose control of yourself) is khamr, from the word khamara, which means 'to cover'. Anything that 'covers' or affects the mind is not allowed. Drugs, such as marijuana, heroin, cocaine and opium are forbidden. Any drug that acts as an escape from the realities of life, produces hallucinations and affects decision making is strictly forbidden. The penalty for taking illegal drugs in an Islamic country is a public flogging. The taking of performance enhancing drugs is seen as cheating and dishonourable.

? Questions

1 What does the term 'haram' mean?
2 Why do Muslims encourage people to give up smoking?
3 Explain what Muslims teach about drinking alcohol.
4 What do Muslims mean when they say that powerful intoxicants are khamr?
5 Explain the attitude of Muslims towards illegal drugs.

For discussion

1 'Smoking is more dangerous than alcohol, so Muslims ought to prohibit the use of both.' Do you agree? Give reasons. C2.1a

2 'It must be hard being a Muslim in Britain and not being allowed to drink.' Do you agree? Give reasons.

Aim

To understand Jewish teachings and beliefs concerning drug abuse.

In Judaism, health is a religious concern and may not be overlooked. Judaism prizes the sanctity of life and Jews are taught that our bodies are on loan from God and that we have a responsibility to preserve and protect them.

Smoking

There is more than one opinion in Judaism concerning whether smoking should be permitted or prohibited. Certainly smoking is not encouraged because of the dangers of lung cancer and other illnesses. Many rabbis would like to see it banned whereas some suggest a compromise, such as prohibiting smoking in public places where non-smokers would be affected and not smoking on the Sabbath. Many Jews do smoke, although the numbers are declining. Many rabbis believe that it is important to encourage young people not to take up the habit.

Alcohol

It is recognized in Judaism that too much drinking clouds judgment and causes people to do things that normally they would not do.

> *'Drinking too much makes you loud and foolish. It's stupid to get drunk.'*
>
> (Proverbs 20: 1)

In the Talmud it says that a rabbi may not give judgement if he has been drinking and some of the passages in the TeNaKh appear to criticize heavy drinking.

> *'You are doomed! You get up early in the morning to start drinking, and you spend long evenings getting drunk.'*
>
> (Isaiah 5: 11)

At the same time, drinking alcohol is part of the Jewish tradition. Wine is drunk to celebrate the Sabbath and festivals like Pesach. At the festival of Purim the Talmud instructs Jews to get a little tipsy so that they are hardly certain if they are 'blessing Mordechai or cursing Haman'.

Illegal drugs

Judaism teaches that it is right to follow the law of the land (providing it does not stop Jews following the law of their religion). As a result, if certain drugs are classed as illegal, their use in Jewish law is also wrong.

Drug abuse and performance enhancing drugs are forbidden in the Jewish tradition because Jews are not allowed to:

- destroy their own body, which the use of illegal drugs can certainly do

- endanger their own lives, and many illegal drugs are very dangerous

- inflict damage upon other people, which supplying drugs does.

Self-abuse, such as injecting drugs, is totally unacceptable, as each person has a responsibility to treat their body with respect. Jews believe that taking drugs to improve performance in sport is dishonest and a danger to health. To use drugs that affect the mind is also thought of as inappropriate as it affects reasoning and judgement.

? Questions

1 Explain Jewish attitudes towards smoking.
2 Why do Jews say that it is wrong to drink too much?
3 What is the Jewish attitude towards drinking at a celebration?
4 Explain Jewish attitudes towards illegal drugs.

For discussion

'If getting drunk is acceptable on one occasion during the year it should be allowed at other times.' Do you agree? Give reasons. Citizenship 2b

Buddhism

Aim
To understand Buddhist teachings and beliefs concerning drug abuse.

The Buddhist religion emphasizes the importance of wisdom. Intoxicants, such as alcohol, cigarettes and drugs, are harmful to health, and those who take them lose their wisdom. On the surface it may seem that the person taking them is not hurting other people. Buddhists argue that if we become drunk, or if we are under the influence of drugs, we may lose our self-control and do something that might hurt others.

Smoking
Buddhists are encouraged to live in the right way and follow The Eightfold Path. This includes taking Right Action. Smoking is not a right or perfect action because of the damage that it does to the smoker. Also, non-smokers who inhale the smoke have their health put at risk. Offering cigarettes to Buddhist monks would be a wrong action.

Alcohol
The fifth precept is not to take drugs and alcohol that cloud the mind. Most Buddhists do not drink alcohol because of this. Some are prepared to drink a little. Those that do, avoid letting their minds becoming fogged by it, because too much drink prevents Right Mindfulness, part of The Eightfold Path. Buddhists do not believe in trying to hide away from the truth. Drinking should not be a way of trying to escape from life.

The Sigalovada Sutta in the Pali Canon lists six dangers that result from addiction to alcohol. These are:

- loss of wealth
- increase in arguing and quarrels
- increased likelihood of getting disease
- loss of good character
- immoral behaviour
- lessening of intelligence.

These are dangers that Buddhists try to avoid.

Illegal drugs
Anyone breaking the fifth precept is quite likely to break all the other precepts along with it, as they are not fully aware of what they are doing. Buddhists emphasize the need to be alert in body, speech and mind in order to think about the consequences of their actions and be able to meditate properly. Addicts use illegal drugs to get away from the truth and this is not acceptable.

Drug dealing is considered to be wrong because it involves harming others. Drugs are permitted for medical use but what is forbidden is drug abuse. Taking drugs to improve performances in sport is not a right action as it involves cheating. Non-medical use of drugs is thought of as poisoning the body.

? Questions
1. How do you think a Buddhist would answer a person who says, 'It's my body, why can't I do what I want with it? I'm not harming anyone else'?
2. Explain why it would be wrong to offer cigarettes to a Buddhist monk.
3. Explain the six dangers that, according to the Sigalovada Sutta, result from being addicted to alcohol.
4. What does the fifth precept say about alcohol and drugs?
5. The Eightfold Path includes Right Action and Right Mindfulness. How would a Buddhist who gets addicted either to drink or drugs be breaking them?

For discussion
'Surely there is nothing wrong in letting your hair down and getting drunk on a Saturday night. It's only escaping the realities of life for a little while.' How far do you agree? Give reasons.
C2.1a; Citizenship 2c

Aim
To understand Hindu teachings and beliefs concerning drug abuse.

Within Hindu society, the use of some drugs in a non-medical way is not considered inappropriate. It is often difficult to separate Hindu beliefs and teachings from the culture of the society in which Hindus live.

Smoking

Many Hindus in India today are smokers. This is partly because they have copied smoking from western society and tobacco companies have used the opportunity to make sales. Many Indians, particularly in rural areas, chew tobacco. However, Hinduism does not encourage the use of substances that have a harmful effect on health. Hindu teaching is opposed to smoking, which is banned at Hindu temples.

Alcohol

In several Indian states alcohol abuse is a problem. Laws have been passed to try to control too much drinking. Hindu teaching does not agree with alcohol abuse, as it causes people to lose control and do evil things. Alcohol addiction is seen as preventing spiritual progress.

'All those which produce molasses and such intoxicants are to be forbidden by those who desire spiritual rewards.'

(Manusmriti)

Illegal drugs

Some Hindus believe that in the Indian tradition marijuana is associated with immorality. They say that when the gods, helped by demons, churned the ocean to obtain Amrita, the elixir (potion) of eternal life, one of the resulting nectars was cannabis. After churning the ocean, the demons tried to gain control of Amrita (marijuana), but the gods prevented them and gave cannabis the name Vijayal (victory) to celebrate their success.

A Hindu legend concerning the God Shiva says that he had a family quarrel and went out to the fields. To shelter from the sun he sat under a hemp plant and he felt so refreshed from the hemp plant that it became his favourite food. As a result he was given the title Lord of Bhang. Some Hindu ascetics (holy men) view bhang (a drink made from hemp leaves) as the giver of long life and a means of communicating with the divine spirit in worship. Some Hindus including sages have taken drugs for meditative purposes.

Many Hindus are opposed to any intoxicating or addictive drugs. They believe that Hindu sacred writings totally forbid the use of illegal drugs and anything that will affect the mind or cause dangers to the health of the individual.

'Bewildered by numerous thoughts, entangled in the web of delusion and addicted to the ratification of desires (like consuming intoxicants) the stupid people fall into a foul hell.'

(Bhagavad Gita)

In practice, some Hindus consider the moderate use of drugs to be acceptable. This does not apply to sport. To take performance enhancing drugs is cheating.

? Questions

1 Explain Hindu beliefs and teaching concerning alcohol abuse.
2 Give some examples of stories associated with drugs in Hindu mythology.
3 Explain why some Hindus are totally opposed to the use of illegal drugs.

For discussion

'Taking substances that give mystical experiences goes against the beliefs Hindus have about how life should be.' Do you agree? Give reasons.
Citizenship 3a

Aim
To understand Sikh teachings and beliefs about drug abuse.

Sikhs regard the body as a temple built by God. So each person should respect their body and do nothing to harm it. It should not be changed by the use of non-medical drugs.

Smoking

Sikhs are not allowed to smoke. Smoking is listed in the Reht Maryada (Code of Conduct) as one of the four sins (Kurahits). It is said that Guru Gobind Singh was once riding his horse with a group of Sikhs and he suddenly stopped. He dismounted and pulled up a wild tobacco plant. Asked why he had done such a thing, he replied that Sikhs should avoid alcohol as it destroys a generation, but tobacco destroys several generations. By this, the Guru meant that smoking is more dangerous than alcohol and he told his followers not to use tobacco.

Alcohol

The Reht Maryada states that Sikhs should not use intoxicants such as drugs or alcohol. The Guru Granth Sahib also makes it clear that Sikhs should not drink alcohol because it leads people to do wrong things.

> 'The body is the pitcher, selfhood the wine;
> And society is of craving and outgoing of the mind.
> Yes, Desire is drinking bowl brimming over with falsehood;
> And Yama is the bar-man.
> Drinking such a wine, who can earn anything but vice and sin.'
>
> (Adi Granth: 553)

> 'By drinking wine one loses sanity and becomes mad, loses the power of discrimination and incurs the displeasure of God.'
>
> (Adi Granth: 554)

The mind should be kept clear to do God's will and not be clouded by the use of alcohol. For those who know God it should not be necessary to drink alcohol.

> 'Why should one who deals in the nectar of God's name develop love for mere wine?'
>
> (Adi Granth: 360)

Illegal drugs

In the time of Guru Nanak it was quite usual for drugs to be used. When offered a drink that contained opium, Guru Nanak remarked that it was more important to be 'hooked' on praising God.

To a Sikh it is important to maintain control over the senses and not to lose the power to reason. Intoxication means that people are not aware of their actions and cannot tell the difference between good and bad. All substances, which are harmful physically or mentally, are banned.

> 'Intoxicated with opium, cannabis and alcohol people forget good deeds and … wander in the life of confusion.'
>
> (Bhai Gurdas Ji: 3916)

The Nihangs of Punjab, who are the defenders of the historic Sikh shrines, are an exception. They take cannabis to help in meditation.

The emphasis of Sikhs on physical fitness rules out illegal drug taking. The following extract from the letter of Baba Banda Bahadur, dated 12 Sammat 1667, sums up the Sikh view: '… *Cannabis, tobacco, opium, poppy seeds, alcohol and any other intoxicants must not be consumed …*'

? Questions

1 What does the Reht Maryada say about smoking?
3 Explain why Sikhs consider it wrong to drink alcohol.
3 Explain Sikh attitudes towards taking illegal drugs.

For discussion

Guru Gobind Singh appears to have believed that smoking is more dangerous than alcohol abuse. Do you agree? Give reasons. C2.1a

Aims

To review a summary of the important issues concerning religious attitudes to drug abuse and to study some exam questions.

Now that you have considered the difficult religious issues on drug abuse, it is time to see if you can answer the type of question that will appear in exams. Before you do so, have a look at the factfile summary to check how much you know.

Factfile summary

I need to make sure that I:

- know and understand religious attitudes towards drug abuse, including its physical, mental and spiritual consequences.

- understand religious beliefs about the value of human life and the attitudes towards the mind and physical body.

- know the meaning of the following terms: hard and soft drugs, non-medical use of drugs, performance enhancing drugs, recreational drugs and social drugs.

- understand the effect of different legal and illegal drugs upon the human body and mind.

- know the legal status of different drugs.

- understand why people take illegal drugs.

- can evaluate the arguments for and against legalizing drugs.

Exam questions

1 a Explain some of the reasons people give for taking drugs. [5 marks]

   b Explain religious attitudes towards alcohol and illegal drugs. [10 marks]

   c 'The law should not get involved in personal matters like taking drugs.' How far do you agree? Give reasons for your answer, showing that you have thought about more than one point of view. Refer to religious teachings in your answer. [5 marks]

2 a Give an outline of what the law says about 'soft' and 'hard' drugs. [5 marks]

   b How might the teachings of the religion(s) you have studied affect the attitudes of believers towards drug taking in sport? [10 marks]

   c 'Cigarettes come with a health warning. Alcohol and caffeine need one too.' How far do you agree? Give reasons for your answer, showing that you have thought about more than one point of view. Refer to religious teachings in your answer. [5 marks]

3 a Outline the ways in which drug addicts may suffer as a result of their addiction. [5 marks]

   b Explain religious attitudes towards smoking tobacco and cannabis. [10 marks]

   c 'You should be able to use any drug so long as you aren't hurting anybody else.' How far do you agree? Give reasons for your answer, showing that you have thought about more than one point of view. Refer to religious teachings in your answer. [5 marks]

What is the media?

> ### Aim
> To understand:
> - the meaning of the term 'media'
> - how access to media has increased
> - religion in relation to media and technology. Citizenship1g

The media

When we talk about the media, what we are referring to is how we obtain our information – newspapers, magazines, television, cinema, music and, more recently, the Internet. These media have an enormous influence on our lives. By the end of the twentieth century over 98 per cent of British households had a television and more than half of families with children had a computer. In the year 2000, 17.9 million of the British population had access to the Internet. That's 7.8 million households.

Television

We spend more than a third of our lives asleep. The next most time-consuming activity is watching television! Recent surveys have shown that on average people aged four and over watch television for 25 hours a week. For many people, the latest events in the more popular soaps are a popular topic of conversation.

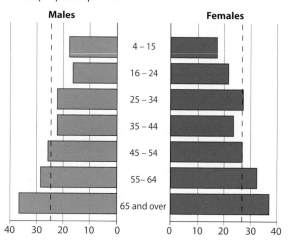

United Kingdom
Hours per person per week

Television viewing by gender and age, 1998

Cinema

The popularity of the cinema has varied considerably over the years. There was a decline in its popularity from 1950–89, matched by the rise in the number of people who owned televisions. During the 1990s, the cinema industry spent millions of pounds on changing its image. Single-screen, dingy cinemas were replaced by clean, smart, multi-plex centres. Cinemas now offer a wide choice of films along with food bars and reasonably priced seats. As a result, there were 142.5 million cinema admissions in the year 2000 as watching films once more became fashionable.

The Press

Newspapers and magazines are easily available and are read by millions of people every day. They are often described as either 'tabloid' or 'broadsheet', because of their shape and size. The Audit Bureau of Circulations (ABC) publishes figures that tell us how many people are reading which papers. The Bureau describes them as 'popular', 'mid-market' and 'quality'. The figures for a single day in March 2001 show that over 14 million national newspapers are read each day.

Title	
National popular morning	
The Mirror	2 189 085
Daily Star	569 883
The Sun	2 514 787
National morning mid-market	
Daily Express	974 714
The Daily Mail	2 403 754
National morning quality	
The Daily Telegraph	1 019 290
The Guardian	399 696
The Independent	225 606
The Times	715 079

Music

It is difficult to over-estimate the influence of the music industry on modern day society, particularly on the teenage sector. In 2000, millions of pounds were spent on CDs, and millions more on associated goods such as T-shirts and posters. The popularity of leading pop and rock stars is reflected in the huge sums they earn and the 'hero-worship' that surrounds them.

Not only the music, but also the lifestyles of pop stars have a huge impact on fashion and teenage behaviour. Obviously, the record companies are keen to promote the image of their stars. The more they are in the news, the more CDs they are likely to sell. But it is not only young people who are keen on music, as is shown by the continued popularity of bands from the 1970s and the vast array of 'tribute bands', such as Abbamania (ABBA) and T-Rextasy (T-Rex).

Religion, the media and technology

The great religions of the world began hundreds or thousands of years ago and the founders and early believers in these religions could never have imagined the lifestyles of people today. We cannot look in sacred writings or the sayings of founders to find reference to our media and technology, but religions themselves increasingly make use of the media and technology for their own purposes. Religious publications, films and TV programmes, are widely used to spread the message of faith.

Satellite transmission means that radio and TV programmes can be broadcast around the world.

The development of the Internet has also had a major impact on how the individual religions can spread their beliefs. Take a look at the Catholic Information Network, to see how the catholic church has embraced the new technology. Other religious groups have gained widespread publicity for their views on current issues through the Internet. A search of the Internet will produce thousands of web sites about religion, spirituality and ethical and moral issues.

? Questions

1. What is meant by the word 'media'?
2. What influence does the media have on our lives?
3. How has the development of the media helped religions spread their message?

For discussion

'The development of the media has done nothing but good for religions.' Do you agree? C1.1a

For research

Look up the BBC's online service. What does it provide on religion? Record your findings. IT2.1

This band was formed after nationwide auditions. The TV programme showing the auditions was watched by millions of viewers

Religious broadcasting on television

Aim

To understand:

- religious broadcasting on the BBC and ITV channels
- the use of satellite broadcasting for evangelism. Citizenship 1g

Religious broadcasting

Religious broadcasting is controlled by The Broadcasting Act, 1990. This requires the BBC, the ITC and the Radio Authority to:

- act responsibly in terms of religious broadcasting
- have respect for listeners and their beliefs
- avoid broadcasting anything which might be offensive towards the views and beliefs of members of a religion or denomination.

Programmes must be accurate and fair and must not misrepresent beliefs and practices. Producers are told that references to religion, including deities, scriptures, holy days and rituals, such as the crucifixion, the Gospels, the Qur'an and the Jewish Sabbath, must be respectful. Religious programmes must not be used for recruiting followers, nor must they seek to persuade or influence listeners by preying on their fears.

Range of programmes

The range of programmes is required to reflect the worship, thought and actions of the mainstream religious traditions in the UK. Most programmes are Christian, but other programmes are aimed at different religious groups.

The BBC is required to broadcast religious programmes. According to its own figures in 2000, it broadcast 600 hours on the radio and 110 hours on television. In addition, in February 2001, the BBC opened its 'Religion and Ethics' website. It has a guide to the six main religions of the world and includes news, comments, an Internet discussion group and links to other sites. It also covers ethical and spiritual issues, provides a calendar of religious festivals, and links to its religious broadcasting.

ITV tells its individual Channel 3 licensees that they must provide an average of at least two hours a week of religious programmes, including acts of worship and a range of other programme types. Breakfast-time television must include a weekly reflection slot, coverage of religious festivals and other items within general programming. Channel 4 is not required by the Broadcasting Act to have religious programmes, although it tries to include about one hour a week of religion in peak time. Channel 5 has to provide a minimum of one and half hours of religious broadcasting each week.

Religious Television & Radio on the BBC

RADIO		
Thought for the Day		
• Monday to Saturday	07:45 - 07:48	*Radio 4*
Daily Service		
• Weekdays	09:45 - 10:00	*Radio 4*
Prayer For The Day		
• Weekdays	05:43 - 05:45	
and Saturday	05:45 - 05:47	*Radio 4*
Sunday		
• Sundays	07:10 – 07:55	*Radio 4*
Good Morning Sunday		
• Sundays	07:00 – 09:00	*Radio 2*
Sunday Half Hour		
• Sundays	20:30 – 21:00	*Radio 2*
Sunday Worship		
• Sundays	08:00 – 08:45	*Radio 4*
Sunday Morning		
• Sundays	06:00 – 10:00	*Radio Scotland*
Faith in Mind		
• Saturdays and Sundays		*Radio 4*
Belief		
• Saturday	22:00 - 22:30	*Radio 3*
TELEVISION		
The Heaven and Earth Show		
• Sunday	10:00 – 11:00	*BBC1*
Songs of Praise		
• Sundays	17:30 – 18:05	*BBC1*
Son of God		
• Sundays	21:10	*BBC1*

A typical week's listing of religious prgrammes, on the radio and television

Quality

There has been much debate between leading religious figures and the BBC in recent years over the quality and quantity of religious programmes and the times at which they are shown. Nigel Holmes, a radio producer and Church of England General Synod member, noted in a letter to *The Guardian*,

> 'In 10 years the total output of BBC1 and BBC2 had increased by half – yet hours devoted to religious topics had declined by one third.'

Recently the Director General of the (Jewish) British Board of Deputies, has said,

> 'Religious output? It's a bit thin. There is a growth in interest in society in spiritual matters. But this is not being reflected by the broadcasters.'

In reply, the BBC points out its commitment to religious broadcasting and the number of new religious programmes it continues to produce. It is also very proud of programmes such as 'Songs of Praise', which is shown just after the early evening news on Sundays (a period of time still often referred to as 'The God Slot' because of its association with religious programmes). These debates will continue in the future as religious bodies press for more air-time and television companies balance the various demands of their viewers. Articles about this can be found on *The Guardian's* website.

Televangelism

Currently, religious organizations may not own television broadcast licenses in the UK. This is not the case in other countries, particularly the USA. TV stations dedicated solely to religion have given us the term 'televangelism'. Evangelists are people who spread the teachings of their faith to encourage believers and to convert non-believers.

The USA is considered the home of this sort of broadcasting. Religious groups and sects own many channels there. Most use their programmes for bible study, preaching, televising services and hearing testimonies from believers. These programmes can reach audiences of millions and have a wide following. Religious groups in the UK are watching the situation with interest.

As the number of satellite and digital channels increases, they hope that the government will allow religious groups to hold licenses.

But there are dangers in televangelism. Religious leaders are exposed to the public and any indiscretions quickly publicized. There have been several sexual and financial scandals over the years involving televangelists that have tended to discredit much of what their programmes try to achieve.

? Questions

1 What requirements are placed on TV companies in relation to religious broadcasting?

2 What are the advantages and disadvantages of televangelism?

For discussion

'There should be no religious broadcasting, because whatever is broadcast is bound to offend some faith group.' Do you agree? C1.1a

For research

Go to *The Guardian's* website and look up the most recent reports on religious broadcasting. Record your findings. Citizenship 2a; IT2.1

Controlling the media 1

Aim
To understand the debate on the effects of the media, particularly on children.
Citizenship 1f, g

With the growth of the media many people have become increasingly concerned about its influence on young people. Until recently, parents have been able to exercise a degree of control over what their children read, see or listen to. Technological developments have meant this is no longer possible. Televisions in bedrooms, the spread of videos, portable CD players, increased access to the Internet and the rapid development of mobile phone technology, have taken away much of that control.

An excellent example of this can be seen in the influence the words of some songs may have on vulnerable young people. At least two teenage suicides have been linked to the lyrics of Eminem songs. One father described his daughter as infatuated with the singer. The girl's mother claimed her daughter had developed a fascination with suicide and a 'love affair' with Eminem. In another case, a coroner criticized Eminem's 'depressing' lyrics after a 17-year-old boy had included the words 'rock bottom' in his suicide note.

Television

The use of offensive language, violence and sex scenes, are the most common causes of complaint about TV programmes. Such language is connected with racism, sexual swearwords, name-calling towards people with disabilities, and unnecessary use of religious names such as 'Jesus Christ' or 'God'. The guidelines point out that both violence and sexual behaviour are linked to morality. Producers have to consider the context in which a violent incident takes place, its effect on the viewer at home seeing it for the first time, and the cumulative effect if programmes containing violence are scheduled close together. They should also make sure that TV programmes do not contain anything that is obscene or pornographic and avoid stereotyping and applying different standards to the way they present men and women.

The watershed

The BBC and the commercial stations have a policy that before 9pm their programmes should be suitable for audiences that include children. Parents are expected to decide on the suitability of individual programmes for their children, but before this time care is taken over the language used in programmes and in showing scenes of explicit sex and violence. After the 9pm watershed, warnings have to be given if programmes contain anything that might offend people.

Probably the first and most famous person to express fears about the effects of television was Mary Whitehouse. In 1964, she set up the National Viewers' and Listeners Association (NVALA). She was in no doubt about a connection between what people see and read and the way they behave. As a Christian and a teacher, she believed that television was attacking Christian values and undermining family life.

The NVALA is now known as mediawatch-uk. It continues to believe that the media have undermined society by putting forward degrading values and models of behaviour. However, other people take the view that television only reflects what is happening in society. So, the question is, 'Does television help to create the decline in marriage, the increase in one-parent families and divorce and the rise in sexual offences and sexual promiscuity, or do the programmes that deal with these subjects just show society as it is?'

In 1964, Mary Whitehouse said, 'If violence is shown as normal on TV, it will lead to a violent society.'

Mediawatch-uk believes the media have a moral responsibility to society

Controlling commercial TV and radio

Under the Broadcasting Acts, 1990 and 1996, **The Independent Television Commission** (ITC) is responsible for commercial television companies and The Radio Authority licenses and regulates independent radio services. The ITC monitors what the independent TV companies do and makes sure they keep within the codes and guidelines on programme content, advertising and sponsorship, and technical performance. It also investigates complaints. **The Radio Authority** makes sure, for example, that advertising is 'legal, decent, honest and truthful'. **The Broadcasting Standards Commission** deals with complaints from individuals. For example, people may claim that a programme has treated them unfairly or invaded their private life. It also considers complaints about taste, decency, violence and sexual conduct in programmes and advertisements.

? **Questions**

1 Why is the 'watershed' important?
2 Why did Mary Whitehouse want to 'clean up' TV?

For discussion

'There is far too much bad language, sex and violence on TV.' How far do you agree? C1.1a

For research

Use the Internet to find out more about the work of one of the following:

• The Independent Television Commission

• The Radio Authority

• The Broadcasting Standards Commission. IT1.1

> **Aim**
> To investigate the ways in which the media is
> controlled and its importance. Citizenship 1g

Controlling the press

The freedom of the press is an important part of
our democratic rights. Most people accept that
there has to be a measure of control over what is
published. **The British National Union of
Journalists** (NUJ) defends the freedom of the
press, but also has a system of self-regulation that
sets standards in publishing and deals with
complaints. Amongst other things, journalists
have to report fairly and accurately. They must not
intrude into private grief and distress. They
should only mention personal details about
people if they are relevant to what they are writing
and they must not encourage discrimination,
ridicule, prejudice or hatred.

There have been numerous examples, however, of
tabloid papers breaking the agreed code and much
discussion about whether some details given are
really 'in the public interest' or just included to
add 'spice' to a story. Where the public object to
what has been published they can make
complaints to **The Press Complaints
Commission** (PCC). In 1999, 2445 such
complaints were made.

Some of these complaints were concerned with
matters, such as the use of nudity. This applies in
particular to page 3 models. Many people see
these as demeaning to women (or men), offensive
to readers, and sending the wrong message about
self-respect, sex and the body to young people.
Such material is certainly not in keeping with the
values of the religions you are studying. In
response, the tabloid newspapers would argue
that, 'If you don't want to see them, you don't have
to buy the paper.'

There is some control over more explicit material,
some of which can be sold only in licensed 'adult'
bookshops. The presence of such shops, however,
again challenges the teachings of religions that
sexual activity should take place at least within a

loving relationship and, for most religions, only
within marriage.

Magazines aimed at the teenaged girl can have an
even more direct effect on moral values. Although
intended for the middle to upper end of this age
range, much younger girls often read them. The
'problem pages' of these magazines gives advice on
explicitly sexual matters by 'agony aunts' and
'uncles'. These can often conflict directly with the
religious values of the families of which young
people are a part, as can the lifestyle these
magazines promote of having to look good, be
slim, adore pop stars and follow fashion.

Legal controls on the press

Finding words to describe what people should not
be allowed to read, see and hear has always been
difficult. Nowhere has this proved more so than
with **The Obscene Publications Act, 1959 and
1964**. The Act states that an article is obscene if its
effect might be 'to deprave and corrupt' the people
who are likely to read, see or hear what it contains.
Very few cases are brought under this law because
the offence is difficult to prove. Ultimately, it
depends on what a jury understands by the word
'obscene' and the phrase 'to deprave and corrupt'.
Under **The Telecommunications Act, 1984** it is
also an offence to send 'a message or other matter
that is grossly offensive or of an indecent, obscene
or menacing character'. Similar controls exist for
sending material through the post such as **The
Post Office Act, 1953**.

Controlling films and music

All films shown in the UK have to be a given a
'classification' by the **British Board of Film
Classification** (BBFC). The BBFC works on the
principle that adults should be free to choose what
they see, as long as it remains within the law and is
not likely to be harmful to society. The decisions
made by the Board have no legal standing, but are
normally accepted by local authorities, who
control what is shown at cinemas. No film can be
shown without a certificate and cinema managers
are breaking the law if they allow people to see a
film that does not have the right certificate for
their age group. The classifications are as follows:

Suitable for all

 General viewing, but some scenes may be unsuitable for some children

 Suitable only for 12 years and over

 Suitable only for 15 years and over

 Suitable only for adults

 To be supplied only in licensed sex shops to adults of not less than 18 years

Controlling music is much more difficult as it is extremely hard to exercise control over something that someone listens to. A certain degree of control is held with radio stations who produce 'radio edits' where offensive and sexually explicit lyrics are cut out of the record so that it can be played on the air. In 1990, a labeling system was introduced where 'Parental Advisory: Explicit Lyrics' labels were placed on the covers of the records that may prove offensive to some people. However, it is strictly voluntary for a group to use this sticker and most record companies use them as a warning in order to avoid unnecessary complaints. It is also difficult to decide what are seen as 'explicit lyrics', as this term is rather vague and obscure.

The Internet

A major concern in recent years has been how to control what is on the Internet. Some people are horrified to hear that it is possible to find out how to make bombs, how to develop your own drugs and to find almost unlimited pornography on the Internet. There is no control over what can be posted on the Internet, but downloading some

pornographic material may be illegal in the UK if is subject to **The Child Protection Act, 1978**. This makes it an offence to take indecent photographs of a child under the age of 16, or to involve a child below that age in photographs that are indecent.

There are also problems related to chat rooms. These 'rooms' allow people to talk to total strangers, who may, or may not, be telling the truth about themselves. There are very great dangers in what can be suggested in these rooms, especially if it leads to a meeting with the person. People, but especially young children, can give away a lot of information about themselves without realizing what they are doing, or how the other person might use the information.

? Questions

1 Explain the controls placed on the press.
2 What do you think is meant by the word 'obscene' and the phrase 'to deprave and corrupt'? C1.2; 2.2

For discussion

'It doesn't do anyone any harm if young people sneak into films with an adult classification.' How far do you agree? C1.1, 1.2, 2.1; Citizenship 1g

For research

1 Use the Internet to find out more about the controversy surrounding Eminem. Record your findings. C2.2; Citizenship 2a; IT1.1
2 Draw up a list of guidelines for using Internet chat rooms to make them safer for users. C2.3; Citizenship 2a; IT1.1
3 Go to the mediawatch-uk website. Find out what their latest concerns are. Record our findings. C2.2; Citizenship 2a; IT1.1

Aim

To understand Christian attitudes towards the media and technology.

When Christianity makes the headlines it is usually to do with a moral issue, for example, if the Pope, a bishop, priest or any member of the laity makes a statement that attempts to apply the Christian faith to a particular situation. It could be about abortion, euthanasia, crime and punishment, drugs, wealth and poverty, sex, or any number of matters. Often, comments will be in response to something that somebody else has said or done. The debate may also be between Christians who interpret their beliefs differently.

Christians, however, look to the media to uphold and support the basic values of the faith. They share with members of other religions concerns about many aspects of life today. Some believe the media have done much to challenge and weaken traditional Christian values to do with the sanctity of life, marriage and the family, and respect for God and the Church. They believe that once the values which hold society together have been taken away, then it is no surprise that violence, drug abuse, criminal activity, pornography and sexual promiscuity take over.

Blasphemy

The criminal law still protects Christianity, and specifically the Church of England, to a certain extent. In 1979, the magazine *Gay News* was charged with blasphemy for printing a poem by James Kirkup, 'The love that dares to speak its name.' The poem describes the love of a homosexual soldier for the dead Christ. On that occasion, blasphemy was defined as '*any contemptuous, reviling, scurrilous or ludicrous matter relating to God, Jesus Christ or the Bible*'. The judge ruled that '*it is not blasphemous to speak or publish opinions hostile to the Christian religion*' as long as the '*the tone, style and spirit*' are '*decent and temperate*'. Gay News was found guilty. The poem was banned and it is still illegal to print it in England. However, in 1997 the police decided not to bring charges against the Lesbian and Gay Christian

Movement, whose website provided a link to the poem through a US Internet site.

A similar situation arose when the British Board of Film Classification refused to give a classification certificate to the film *Visions of Ecstasy*, about St Theresa of Avila. The film included sexual imagery focused on the figure of the crucified Christ. If the male figure had not been Christ, the film would have been given an 18 certificate.

Christians, however, do not make a habit of protecting their faith in this way. The previous successful blasphemy trial was in 1922. Referring to the law on blasphemy, John Patten (Minister of State at the Home Office, 1989) said, '*The Christian faith, no longer relies on it, preferring to recognize that the strength of their own belief is the best armour against mockers and blasphemers.*'

Newspapers, the Internet and satellite broadcasting

In April 2000, the *Guardian* reported the Archbishop of York as saying that the Internet could lead to a '*soulless society*' and that it has potential for evil as well as good. The Archbishop of Canterbury similarly was also quoted as saying that it can be a '*tool of empowerment. But it can also be exclusive and isolating*'. They are both concerned that people could become increasingly cut off from each other and begin to live in a virtual world rather than the real world. The freedom to create and post websites also provides the opportunity for extremists and dangerous cults to publicize themselves.

Nevertheless, today many Christian groups use the latest technology to spread their message around the world. Evangelism from the pulpit reaches a few people; on television and in newspapers it can reach millions, but on the Internet it can reach the world.

Trinity Broadcasting Network (TBN) is believed to be the world's largest Christian network. It was started in 1973 and has 536 broadcasting stations around the world. The Christian Broadcasting Network (CBN) is one of the largest Christian broadcasting television ministries. Its programmes are broadcast across the USA and to 90 other countries. It had a mission to convert five million people to Christianity by 2000.

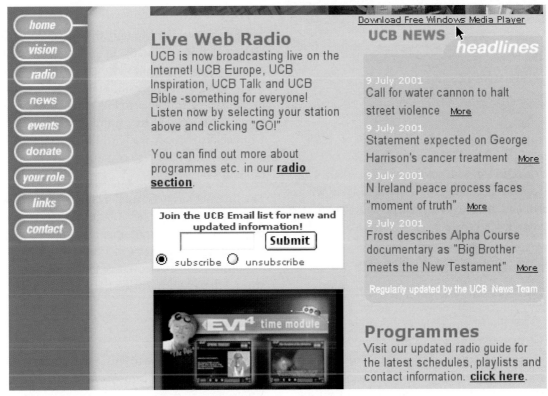

United Christian Broadcasters set up the first Christian radio station in the UK

Most of these developments in evangelism have taken place in the USA. In the UK such movements are limited and confined to radio, because religious organizations are not allowed to own television broadcast licenses. *United Christian Broadcasters* (UCB) provides '*Christian radio for the nation*'. The other main Christian radio service is *Premier*. Most religious newspapers now have an online edition. Examples include *The Catholic Herald, The Church Times, The Christian Herald* and *The Methodist Recorder*. The Internet also provides prayer sites, such as Praying Each Day and Bible search facilities such as The Bible Gateway.

❓ Questions

1 What are some basic Christian values?

2 What concerns do some Christians have about the media?

3 What is blasphemy?

4 What concerns do some Christians have about the Internet?

5 What are the advantages of modern technology for spreading Christianity?

📺 For discussion

1 As a class or group, choose one TV programme this week that you will all watch. Look at it from the point of view of Christian values. Discuss how the programme shows scenes that Christianity would find unacceptable. C2.1a

2 'The law on blasphemy should either be abolished or be applied to all religions.' How far do you agree? C1.1,2.1; Citizenship 2b,c

◆ For research

1 Search one of the online newspapers listed opposite to find out what is in the Christian news. See if you can find any articles about other topics you study for this subject. Citizenship 2a; IT 2.1

2 Go to The Bible Gateway site and choose a word from a topic you have studied. Copy and paste your findings. IT 2.1

Aim
To understand Muslim attitudes towards the media and technology.

Muslims submit themselves to the will of **Allah**. They do their best to live their lives in accordance with the **Qur'an**, which is the word of Allah. They also look to the sayings of Muhammad, known as **Hadith** and to **Sunnah**. These, taken together provide the law of Islam, are known as **Shari'ah**.

Blasphemy

Muslims look to the media to uphold the beliefs, teachings and moral values of Shari'ah. In countries where Islam is the main religion, the law is often used to protect the faith. Where Muslims live in countries where Islam is not the main religion, they do not have the same safeguards. In Pakistan, for example, blasphemy is punishable by death. In England, however, an attempt in 1988 to have the author, Salman Rushdie, and publishers of *The Satanic Verses* charged with blasphemy failed because English law applies only to Christianity. However, the case drew attention to how seriously Muslims view anything that shows disrespect for Islam. In February 2000, Salman Rushdie was still receiving police protection twelve years after the late Ayatollah Khomeni of Iran issued a fatwa, or religious ruling, calling for his death. This ruling was lifted in 1998. Filmmakers, however, have respected the Muslim command never to represent the Prophet Muhammad in any way.

Moral values

Muslims share the concerns of many religious people about the moral values that the media sometimes put forward. They are particularly concerned about the effects on young people who grow up in the UK away from the controls of a Muslim society. Smoking, drinking alcohol, drug taking, violence, immodesty, sexual promiscuity, adultery and homosexuality are all contrary to Muslim values. However, when Muslims watch the television and read the newspapers they are often presented with these as acceptable parts of everyday life.

Using the media

Muslims appreciate, though, that much good can also come from the media in terms of education and in widening people's knowledge. Radio has made possible local Muslim stations that broadcast programmes in English and other languages to serve their communities. Radio Ummah also broadcasts worldwide via the Internet. Its website also contains many useful links.

The Internet has been used by many Muslims as a way of promoting Islam. A large number of sites contain the Qur'an and other teachings of Islam. Many also present the news from a Muslim perspective and give coverage to items from around the Muslim world.

? Questions

1 How did some Muslims react to the publication of *The Satanic Verses*?

2 What are the main concerns of Muslims about the media?

3 How have Muslims made use of developments in media and technology?

For discussion

'The law in the UK should protect all religions, not just Christianity.' How far do you agree? C2.1a

For research

1 Several websites have online versions of newspapers and magazines or provide opportunities for discussion. The content of these is always changing. Search on one of the following to find out what is in the Muslim news at the moment:

- Islam City covers news, media and the faith, with many links and a sound recording of the Qur'an with translations.

- The Modern Religion contains a summary of key beliefs in different sections with lots of links.

- *The Muslim News* online. IT2.1

Aim
To understand Jewish attitudes towards the media and technology.

Developments in the media and technology have increased access to knowledge and ideas. Generally, therefore, Jews have welcomed these. They make it possible to listen to different points of view and understand more about the world. There is a great tradition of debate within Judaism. Throughout history Jews have had to interpret their laws to meet new circumstances and different situations. This is reflected in the **Talmud**, which contains many discussions about the meaning of commandments contained in the **Torah** and how they should be applied to everyday life.

Moral values

The Jewish faith focuses on respect for God and His laws, the value of life and the importance of the family. Jews, like members of other religions, also have their concerns about the media. The violence, sexual misconduct and abuse and devaluing of family life which forms a part of TV programmes and films goes against all the teachings of Judaism.

Representing Judaism

Jews also have a special interest in how they and their beliefs are represented in the media. As a minority group that has been persecuted in the past, they are aware of the dangers of stereotyping, even through comedy. They are also concerned about how political issues in Israel and the Middle East are described. There is also a feeling amongst some Jews that the limited amount of time given to religious programmes on TV means that their own faith is often poorly represented. Others feel there could be more programmes about Jewish life and culture if broadcasters didn't classify them as 'religious'. In February 2001, *The Guardian* quoted a spokesman for the organization as saying, '*There are 30 000 Jewish people in the UK … and we don't feel our needs are being addressed.*'

The group would like to see at least 20 hours a year given to Jewish programmes. Jewish organizations have been quick to make use of the Internet to transmit news and views. For a religion whose members are in communities all around the world this is a powerful way of keeping in touch with what is going on.

? Questions

1 Why have Jews generally welcomed developments in the media and technology?
2 What are the main concerns of Jews about the media?
3 What is stereotyping?
4 What would you include in a series of TV programmes about Jewish life and culture?

For discussion

1 'Jokes about race and religion are funny.' How far do you agree? C2.1a
2 'Television programmes too often present minorities as stereotypes.' How far do you agree? Give examples. C2.1a

For research

1 Find out about Judaism in the religion section of the BBC website and record your findings. IT1.1

2 Several websites have online versions of newspapers and magazines or provide opportunities for discussion. The content of these is always changing. Search on one of the following to find out what is in the Jewish news at the moment:

- The Jewish Community and Totally Jewish both have 'Ask the Rabbi' sections and news.
- *The Jewish Chronicle*, 'the world's leading, and oldest Jewish newspaper'. IT2.1

Buddhism

> ## Aim
> To understand Buddhist attitudes towards the media and technology.

The attitudes of Buddhists are based on their understanding of life or the nature of existence. This is contained in **The Four Noble Truths**, **The Eightfold Path**, and **The Five Precepts**. It is up to individual Buddhists to interpret these for themselves and make their own judgements about matters.

Moral values

There are many issues Buddhists might raise about the production of TV programmes, films and the material that appears on the Internet and in newspapers. Much of what we see in the media supports the Buddhist view that life is full of suffering. Some TV documentaries and discussion programmes also help people to have a better understanding of contemporary issues so that they can make informed decisions about them.

Not all media output can be interpreted so positively, however. Many Buddhists would ask questions about what lies behind the material we see and read. Why is this programme being made? What is the intention or purpose behind it? Does it show an accurate understanding of life? Will it help me along the path to Enlightenment?

Many of the programmes on television are obviously not in keeping with Buddhist values. Although the producers of programmes would usually say they are just showing life as it is, there is always the danger that people copy what they see. In terms of The Five Precepts, many programmes rely on entirely the opposite of what they say:

* murder and violence is the main theme of many films and series
* theft is an equally popular theme
* abusive sexual relationships can often be seen
* the language that is heard and the arguments between characters in soaps, films and crime series is often far away from the idea of Right Speech

* the misuse of alcohol and other drugs features frequently.

In defence of most programmes, those who do wrong usually have to face the consequences of their actions. For many it involves arrest and imprisonment. For others their personal lives suffer in a variety of ways. Producers may rely on the Three Evils of greed, hatred and ignorance for much of the content of their programmes, but they usually show the ultimate triumph of good.

Using the media

Buddhists also realize that the media is a powerful tool for enabling people to find out about their faith. The Dalai Lama, the leader of the Tibetan Buddhists, has made use of the media to draw the world's attention to the problems of his people since the Chinese invasion of Tibet. There are also many sites on the Internet where people can learn about Buddhism.

> ### ❓ Questions
> 1 How do television programmes show different types of suffering?
> 2 How do television programmes go against The Five Precepts?

🗨 For discussion

1 Is working in the media in keeping with the idea of Right Livelihood? C2.1a

2 'Greed, hatred and ignorance are the basis of most TV programmes.' How far do you agree? C2.1a

◆ For research

1 Find out about Buddhism in the religion section of the BBC's website and record your findings. IT2.1

2 Compare the Friends of the Western Buddhist Order site with that belonging to Dharma the Cat. What are the advantages of these two different ways of presenting Buddhism? IT2.1

Aim

To understand Hindu attitudes towards the media and technology.

As Hinduism has no central source of authority, it is up to the individual or groups to decide their attitude to the many issues they face in the modern world. This is true in India, but even more so for those Hindus who have moved to live in the west. Many now have children who were born in the UK. These children may have little or no experience of their religion's home country. However, there are values by which Hindus would try to live their lives. These have been handed down from one generation to the next and may have come from some of the ancient scriptures of Hinduism. In The Laws of Manu, for example, it is stated:

'Non-violence, truthfulness, abstention from unlawfully taking what belongs to others, purity, and control of one's organs, Manu has declared these to be the sum total of the dharma of the four castes.'

Attitudes towards the media and technology need to be seen in the light of such values.

Broadcasting Hinduism

From 6 January to 3 February 2001, Channel 4 broadcast 23 programmes on the Kumbh Mela, a huge festival of life held in Allahabad, India. A Channel 4 spokesperson said, *'We want to bring this international phenomenon and cultural spectacle to life.'* Within a few days of starting their broadcasts, however, the Channel 4 crew had themselves become the subject of a major news item. Many Hindus saw their presence at the festival as an intrusion. Some sadhus (holy men) alleged that meat and alcohol were being provided for the crew, which, they claimed, offended Hindu values.

The sacred writings of the Mahabharata and Ramayana, with their battles between good and evil and their love stories, have made excellent film material. Bombay, in India, is the largest film-producing city in the world, and is often called 'Bollywood' after Hollywood in the USA. In England the Mahabharata has been seen on stage and as a TV serial.

The BBC has an Asian Network on radio and both the BBC and commercial channels have special programmes for the Asian community. Satellite channels, such as Zee Television and Asianet, broadcast in Hindi, English and Indian regional languages. Developments in technology mean that the Asian communities around the world now have access to channels and programmes made especially for them.

? Questions

1 What values are referred to in The Laws of Manu?
2 Why did some sadhus criticize the televising of the Kumbh Mela?
3 Why have the Mahabharata and Ramayana proved so popular as film material?

For discussion

1 What are the problems associated with televising religious events? C2.1a
2 'Stories from sacred writings should not be made into entertainment.' How far do you agree? C2.1a

For research

1 Find out about Hinduism in the religion section of the BBC website or at The Hindu Universe: The Hindu Resource Centre and record your findings. IT2.1a
2 Several websites have online versions of newspapers and magazines or provide opportunities for discussion. The content of these is always changing. Search on one of the following to find out what is in the Hindu news at the moment:

- *Hinduism Today.*
- *The Hindu,* India's national paper. IT2.1

Sikhism

Aim
To understand Sikh attitudes towards the media and technology.

Sikhs have long understood the importance of the media. In 1899, Bhai Vir Singh founded the weekly paper, *Khalsa Samacar* (*News of the Khalsa*). It is still published today in Amritsar. At a time when Sikhs were under attack from Hindus and the English he used the power of the written word to unite his people. Sikhs have continued this tradition through the Internet, where you will find many websites concerned with the faith and its people. The Internet and satellite TV are now an important means of keeping members of the Sikh community around the world in touch. They also allow them to present their own perspectives on issues and focus on particular concerns of Sikhs, such as the Punjab. Many Sikh radio stations broadcast on the Internet. Some Sikhs have set up their own personal websites to promote their faith, for example, Gurpal Singh Samra has his own site.

Moral values
Sikhs believe religious observance and moral behaviour are very important. They draw inspiration from their sacred writings and also the Reht Maryada. This is the Official Sikh Code of Conduct. Like members of other religions, Sikhs look to the media to encourage young people to value marriage and family life and to steer them away from smoking, too much alcohol, drug taking, violence, immodesty, sexual promiscuity and adultery. Very often, however, the opposite is the case and Sikhs become concerned that the media actually have a bad influence on people.

Monitoring the media
Sikhs, like other people, want to see responsible reporting in the media. In 1996, the Sikh Mediawatch And Resource Task Force (SMART) was founded in the USA. Among other things it aims to:

- monitor the media for misinformation and misrepresentation of the Sikh faith and its followers, and to correct errors.

- serve as a source of accurate information on all aspects of the Sikh religion and its followers.

The organization believes the '*Sikh American community has an important contribution to make to all aspects of society, and that this will be promoted by accurate media coverage*'.

❓ Questions
1 Who was Bhai Vir Singh?
2 What is the Rahit Maryada?
3 Give some examples of Sikh values.
4 What does The Sikh Mediawatch And Resource Task Force do?

💬 For discussion
1 'Newspapers are still the best source of information.' How far do you agree? C2.1a

2 'There is no such thing as unbiased reporting.' How far do you agree? Give examples. C2.1a

◆ For research
1 Find out about Sikhism in the religion section of the BBC website and record your findings. IT2.1

2 Several websites have online versions of newspapers and magazines or provide opportunities for discussion. The content of these is always changing. Search on one of the following to find out what is in the Sikh news at the moment:

- Sikh Mediawatch provides coverage of items about Sikhism in the media.

- *The Sikh Review.*

- *Sikh Spirit,* a magazine produced in England. IT2.1

Aim

To review a summary of the important issues concerning religious attitudes to media and technology and to study some exam questions.

Now that you have considered the difficult issues concerning the media and technology, it is time to see if you can answer the type of question that will appear in exams. Before you do so, have a look at the factfile summary to check how much you know.

Factfile summary

I need to make sure that I:

• know what is meant by the media.

• understand about the media in terms of newspapers, magazines, television, cinema, music, the Internet and satellite communication.

• understand the debate about the effects of the media, particularly on children and can give examples.

• understand the possible dangers of everyone being able to use the media.

• understand the debate about controlling the media, including advertising standards, the classification of films, censorship and the TV 'watershed', particularly when it comes to sex, violence and pornography.

• understand the law governing the media and what is meant by self-regulation as it relates to these matters.

• understand what blasphemy means and the laws about it.

• understand about religious broadcasting on the BBC and ITV channels and can give examples.

• understand about the use of satellite broadcasting for evangelism and can give examples.

Exam questions

1 a Explain the concerns that religious people might have about tabloid newspapers.
[5 marks]

   b Explain why religious parents might control the television viewing of their children.
[10 marks]

   c 'The media ignore people's spiritual needs.' How far do you agree? Give reasons to support your answer and show that you have thought about different points of view.
[5 marks]

2 a Explain what is meant by:

      i   blasphemy

      ii censorship.   [5 marks]

   b Explain why some religious people think the law should protect their faith.
[10 marks]

   c 'The Internet is dangerous because it cannot be controlled.' How far do you agree? Give reasons to support your answer and show that you have thought about different points of view.
[5 marks]

3 a Explain two moral values that religious people might like the media to promote.
[5 marks]

   b Explain how the Internet has helped to bring religion to people.   [10 marks]

   c 'Television programmes have a bad effect on young people.' How far do you agree? Give reasons to support your answer and show that you have thought about different points of view.   [5 marks]

Aim

To investigate:

- what is meant by crime
- the causes of criminal actions.
  Citizenship 1a, c

What is crime?

A crime is the breaking of the state law, for example, murder. Some crimes are committed against a person, for example, slander, mugging, committing grievous bodily harm and neglect of children. Other examples of law breaking may involve property, such as theft or fraud. Crimes may also be committed against the country, such as selling state secrets to an enemy or failure to declare earnings and pay taxes.

There are two kinds of offence:

- Non-indictable – these are less serious offences, for example, motoring offences and petty theft.

- Indictable – these are the most serious kinds of crime, such as rape and murder.

Religion and crime

A sin is the breaking of religious moral law. It is possible to sin without committing a crime, for example, being guilty of pride. Each religion has its own religious rules and laws. If religious leaders run a country, then the religious law and the law of the government might be the same, for example, in Afghanistan, but such a situation is unusual.

Although the Church of England is the established church of Britain, religious laws and state laws are separate. Parliament has passed many laws that are based on religious principles, but the two are separate.

Religious offence varies from religion to religion, but include such things as blasphemy (insulting God or sacred things) and the making of images of God.

Crimes in Britain

The number of reported crimes in Britain is on the increase. Since the end of World War I in 1918, recorded crime has increased on average by 5.1 per cent per year. There are now over 5 000 000 reported cases each year.

Is this a true picture of crime in Britain?

It is difficult to say with certainty how much more criminal activity there is today because the way that crime is recorded has changed. For example, since 1998 there has been an attempt to record crime as it affects the victims. If a vandal goes along a street and damages six cars, six separate crimes would be recorded, as six motorists would be affected. Previously, only one offence would have been recorded as one person did it on a single occasion.

Joyriders have stolen this car and then crashed it

Many politicians believe that people are now more prepared to report some types of crime. This includes domestic violence and child abuse. The classification of crime has also changed, for example, 'violence against the person' now includes cruelty and neglect of children. This had the effect of increasing the crimes reported in this category between September 1997 and September 1998 from 240 779 (under old rules) to 524 929.

Causes of crime

Why do people commit offences and break the law? There are several reasons for this, including:

- social reasons, for example, to join in with friends and be one of the 'gang'

- environmental reasons, for example, some criminologists (people who study the causes of crime) believe that poverty and a deprived home background may be an important factor

- psychological reasons, for example, some people believe that human nature is naturally selfish and greedy and that people will always want to have more and be more powerful than others

- drug addiction, for example, some addicts finance their drug habit through shop lifting and prostitution.

Home Office research of the crimes that took place during 2000 showed that around 100 000 persistent offenders (people who keep on committing offences) are responsible for half of the crime in Britain. The crime survey of persistent offenders showed that:

- nearly two-thirds were hard drug users

- half were aged under 21

- three-quarters were unemployed

- half had no educational qualifications

- more than a third were in care as children.

It appears that many people who become involved in crime come from a background that includes poor housing and overcrowding, poverty, unemployment, lack of education, broken homes and drugs. However, these are not the only reasons why people break the law, as the whole issue is very complex.

Psychiatry (the study and treatment of mental disease) generally considers crime to result from emotional disorders that are often linked to childhood experiences. Crimes such as arson that result from pyromania (an uncontrollable urge to set things on fire) or theft that result from kleptomania (an uncontrollable urge to steal things), are thought to be symptoms of personality disorders. Many would argue that crime prevention and the cure of offenders involves treatment not just punishment.

? Questions

1 What is the difference between crime and sin?

2 What is the difference between religious law and state law?

3 Explain what is meant by crimes against:
   a a person
   b property.
   Include examples of each.

4 What reasons are given to explain why there seems to be an increase in law breaking?

5 What reasons are given to explain why people commit offences?

For discussion

1 'Get rid of poverty and drug addiction and you won't have a problem with theft or burglary.' How far do you agree? Give reasons for your opinion. C2.1a

2 'Better education and more contact with the police at school would help to prevent crime.' Make a presentation to the class. C2.1b

For research

1 The Home Office publishes statistics showing the number of crimes that have taken place in Britain each year. Find out the current trends by going to the Home Office website. Record your findings. Include the types of crime that appear to be falling and the ones that are increasing. IT2.1

Punishment and young offenders

Aim
To investigate:
- the aims of punishment
- the treatment of young offenders.
  Citizenship 1a, c

Purpose of punishment

There are five main aims of punishment. Sentences are designed to cover several of the main purposes of punishment.

Protection

The public has the right to feel protected from law-breakers, and punishments, such as imprisonment, are aimed at preventing further criminal actions. People believe that it is far too dangerous to allow some criminals to have their freedom.

Retribution

Many believe that criminals deserve to suffer for what they have done wrong. One of the aims of this type of punishment is to enable the victims to feel that justice has been done. Sometimes this is referred to as 'getting revenge' or 'getting your own back' and may involve the principle of 'an eye for an eye, a tooth for a tooth'.

Deterrence

One aim of punishment is to deter people from committing a crime. Some argue that someone who is thinking of committing murder would not do so if we had the death penalty. Others say that a more severe punishment would deter a potential vandal or thief, but many believe that the only deterrent that is really effective is the certainty of being found out.

Reformation

The aim of this kind of punishment is to show offenders that what they have been doing is wrong. The idea is to help criminals to change their ways, instead of continuing with a life of crime, and persuade them to become responsible citizens. This might involve law-breakers attending group therapy where their crimes are discussed and analyzed, helping the victims of crime, or the carrying out of community service orders (where offenders carry out work to help members of the local community).

Vindication

It is necessary for us, as members of society, to respect the law. Without law and order we could all do whatever we wanted. The result would be total chaos, so one aim of punishment is to make it clear that the law is there to be taken seriously and not to be ignored. Failure to keep the law results in a punishment.

Young offenders

The age of criminality in Britain is 10. This means that once a young person has reached the age of 10, he or she is regarded as old enough to understand right from wrong and can be charged with breaking the law.

Crime among young people is a serious problem in Britain. Young people commit 40 per cent of crimes and in 1998, there were 5283 boys and 302 girls aged under 18 in custody. Reconviction rates for young people leaving custody has always been very high: 88 per cent of 14–16-year-olds released in 1995 were re-convicted within two years. Many argue that this is because they have mixed with other criminals, had their family and education disrupted and have experienced violence and intimidation.

What should be done with young murderers?

In February 1993, Robert Thompson and Jon Venables abducted and murdered a two-year-old boy named James Bulger. These 10-year-olds battered James to death and left him on a Liverpool railway line. In November 1993 their trial took place in Preston. The nation was shocked at such an awful crime and people threw stones at the two police vans taking the boys to court. The crowds shouted abuse, the boys' mothers were verbally attacked and blamed for lack of care, love and firm parental control. Both boys had parents who had separated and had difficulties with attendance, learning and behaviour at school.

The boys were sentenced to be held in secure units, but in October 2000, the Lord Chief Justice ruled that they had served the minimum term necessary for punishment and deterrence. They were to be released and given a new identity and anonymity for life. This caused a public outcry in Liverpool.

In Trondheim, Norway, in 1994, two six-year-old boys stripped a five-year-old girl, stoned her and beat her until she was unconscious. Then they ran away leaving Silje Raedergard in the snow to freeze to death. They had been playing football and the situation had become violent.

How did the people of Trondheim react to such a tragedy? What punishment did they give to the boys? The killing of Silje had a deep effect on the community – they felt grief not only for Silje and her family, but also for the boys and their families. They realized that the boys would have to live with the knowledge of what they had done for the rest of their lives. That was punishment enough and within a few weeks the boys returned to school. There was no public outcry, only sadness, forgiveness and concern. Some would say that the boys were treated more like victims, than killers.

? Questions

1 Explain the five aims of punishment. Include an example of a punishment in each category.

2 Which do you think is the most important aim of punishment? Give your reasons.

3 How much of the national crime, such as theft, burglary, robbery and violence is likely to be committed by young people?

4 Why do you think that so many young people who have been in custody re-offend on release?

For discussion

1 In Norway, the age of criminality is 15, whereas in Britain it is 10. If the James Bulger killing had occurred in Norway, the two 10-year-olds would not have been locked up in a secure unit. Discuss the James Bulger and Trondheim murders. What do you think should have been done in each case? PS2.1

2 At what age do you think people should know right from wrong and be held responsible for their actions? Give reasons.

3 Why do you think that there was such a difference in attitude towards the killers in the two cases?

For research

1 There are organizations that are concerned with the treatment of young offenders. Find out about the work of NACRO and record what it believes should be done to help reduce crime. Use the Internet to obtain extra information. IT2.1

2 Use the Internet to find out more information about young prisoners and record your findings. IT2.1

Types of punishment and the prison system

Aim

To investigate:

- the types of punishments that the courts might use

- the issues concerning Britain's prison system. Citizenship 1a, c

Types of punishment

The type of punishment given depends on the seriousness of the crime. In Britain punishments include the following:

- Custodial sentences, for example prison or detention centres.

- Suspended sentences – these sentences will only take effect if the convicted person is found guilty of another offence within a set time.

- Probation order – offenders have to see a probation officer or attend a probation centre regularly. The task of the probation officer is to 'advise, assist and befriend' the offender and help him or her stay out of trouble.

- Community service orders – offenders are required to do unpaid work for a number of hours varying between 40 and 240 hours.

- Fines – an amount of money paid to the courts, for example, for breaking a traffic law.

Corporal punishment (whipping or caning) and capital punishment (death penalty) are no longer used in Britain.

Prisons

The prison population rose by 50 per cent between 1993 and 1998. By the turn of the century, British jails held more than 60 000 people. The type of criminals varies greatly. In 1995, there were over 4000 prisoners serving life sentences for murder. In the same year, over 20 000 were sentenced to imprisonment for non-payment of fines.

Conditions in prisons vary greatly, but many of the prisons in Britain are full, in some cases there is overcrowding. A report by the Prison Reform

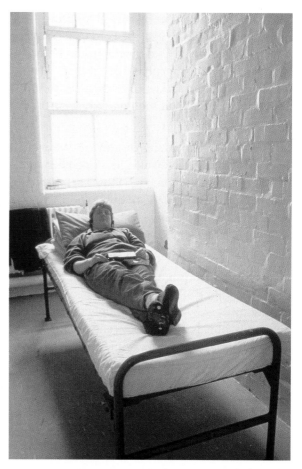

Many prison cells contain the bare minimum of items needed by the prisoner

Trust in January 2001 commented that in Birmingham prison over 750 inmates are crammed two to a one-person cell. In Leeds prison 600 prisoners are doubling up in cells designed for one, and in Preston and Durham the figures are 500 each. Such conditions cause stress to prisoners and between 1986 and 1995, 453 prisoners killed themselves while they were held in custody and in just one year there were 4 778 recorded cases of self-injury in prison. To try to cope with overcrowding there are a number of pre-fab (assembled on site) jails and at Weymouth there is a floating prison (a prison ship).

A report by the Prison Reform Trust claims that youth prisons occupied the worst four positions for prison violence, with an assault rate of over 45 per cent. At Brinsford Young Offender's Institution the rate was 67.5 per cent. In contrast, assault rates in male open prisons average only 2.5 per cent.

Parole

Parole is the temporary or permanent release of prisoners before they have completed their full sentence, on the promise of good behaviour. The rates of release vary for different offences, for example, sex offenders are least likely to be granted parole. The Parole Board carries out interviews and considers the risk to the public of an early release of the prisoner. The board's job is to get the right balance between protecting the public and supervising the return of offenders back into the community. In 1999–2000, 6200 prisoners had their cases reviewed and 2600 were released on parole.

Is prison the best option?

Many people are concerned that too many offenders in Britain receive prison sentences. They say that prison does little to reform a person. Having mixed with other criminals they argue it reinforces criminal tendencies and on release the offender is likely to break the law again. 57 per cent of all prisoners released in 1996 were re-convicted of breaking the law within two years of leaving prison. Among young male offenders this percentage rose to 76 per cent.

Many argue that a major problem with prison sentences is that it isn't just the offender who is punished. When a husband is locked up the wife and children also suffer. Children may be deprived of their mothers at a critical time in their lives if their mothers are behind bars. Many relationships fail to survive the stress and strain of such forced separations.

While in prison the inmates have to make very few choices for themselves. Many prisoners find it very difficult to readjust to life and decision making in the outside world. Some return to crime because they cannot cope with the demands they face. Having to look for a home and a job with a criminal record and no reference is extremely difficult.

Others argue that offenders should be aware of what they have done and that anything less than a prison sentence is being 'soft' on crime. The public needs to be protected from criminals and they should be locked away until they have paid their debt to society. If a person has lost his or her freedom and is in prison he or she cannot continue a life of crime in the community. The other forms of punishment cannot offer such protection and reassurance to the public.

There are organizations, such as the Howard League for Penal Reform and the Prison Reform Trust, which have been set up to campaign for improvements in prison conditions and what they regard as an effective prison system.

? Questions

1 Describe some of the problems of the prison system in Britain.

2 What does the Parole Board have to consider when making decisions about early release?

3 Why do some people say prison is not the best option in reducing crime?

For discussion

1 'The real cause of crime is people choosing to break the law because they think that they can get away with it.' Do you agree? Give reasons.

2 'Bang them up in prison. That'll cut the crime rate.' Do you think this view is true? Give reasons.

3 Find examples of crimes and the punishments given to offenders in the daily newspapers or on TV. In a group, discuss the sentences given. Consider issues such as fairness and the appropriateness of other forms of punishment.

For research

1 Find out more about the aims and the work of organizations that campaign for prison reform. Several Internet sites, such as prison reform and UK online have useful information. IT2.1

2 From your research, give a short talk to the class about the campaign for prison reform. C2.1b

Alternative and capital punishments

Aim
- To investigate punishments that act as an alternative to a prison sentence.
- To examine the arguments for and against capital punishment. Citizenship 1a, c

Electronic tagging

Electronic tagging has been in use in the USA since the 1980s. Electronic ankle tags were first used in Britain in Manchester, Norfolk and Reading during the 1990s. In 1999, the scheme was extended to other parts of Britain. Prisoners will not be considered for this scheme if it is thought that they are a risk to the public, will run off or offend again, or if they have nowhere suitable to live. The idea is to use electronic tagging on prisoners who have been given a prison sentence of less than four years.

The advantage of tagging includes the low cost (currently around £4 a day) and its flexibility. Shoplifters could be kept at home during shop opening hours, and sex offenders who might hang around outside of schools could be kept indoors during the times when students are travelling to or from school. Some argue that the scheme improves the chances of the rehabilitation and the resettlement of offenders into society when they come out of prison. The disadvantages include the technical problems, for example, in one case a 'dead spot' in one offender's house meant that an alarm was triggered although the offender was at home in bed.

Home Detention Curfew scheme

During 1999, nearly 15 000 prisoners were released from prison on to the Home Detention Curfew scheme (HDC). Under this scheme offenders have to agree to stay at home at night. The key factor in making the release decision is whether or not it is thought that the law breaker is likely to continue a life of crime if offered this opportunity to leave prison. Offenders may have to wear an electronic tag linked to a central control unit that monitors offenders and will know if they break the curfew or remove the tag. In 1999, five per cent of offenders who broke the rules were returned to prison.

Community service

One alternative to locking people away is to sentence them to working for the community. Some people see this as a soft option, but others as a way of benefiting the local community and saving money. Clearing areas of derelict land, the restoring of property, the cleaning of rivers and many other worthwhile projects could be carried out by offenders. It costs around £25 000 per year to keep a person in prison, just over £2200 to put someone on probation, but less than £2000 for a community service order.

Capital punishment – the death penalty

Capital punishment or the death penalty has been abolished in over 100 countries including Britain. However, the death penalty is still common in many nations and is usually carried out by hanging or firing squad. A few countries may use lethal injection, such as the USA, China, Guatemala and Taiwan. In Saudi Arabia criminals may be stoned or beheaded. Those countries that execute the most people include China, the Democratic Republic of Congo, the USA and Iran. In the USA there are about 3000 prisoners in prison on death row awaiting execution.

There are many arguments for and against the death penalty.

Arguments against the death penalty

- Sometimes the courts make a mistake. It is claimed that in the USA at least 45 innocent men have been put to death. Proof of their innocence did not come to light until after their execution – then it was too late to put right the injustice.

- There is no evidence that supports the view that the death penalty is more of a deterrent than life imprisonment. Research suggests that most murders are committed when people are under extreme stress or under the influence of drink or drugs. At such a time the murderer is not focusing on the possible consequences of his or her actions.

- Locking someone away for life protects society from the possibility of the person re-offending – there is no need to kill the person.

Should society decide who gets the death penalty?

- Who has the right to execute another person? Many people fear that God may judge them on such an action. Would you be able to sleep at night if you were a hangman and had possibly executed an innocent person?

- Someone who reforms, having once been a serious criminal, can be a powerful influence for good, for example, American gang leader, Nicky Cruz.

Arguments for the death penalty

- The death penalty can act as a deterrent and stop people committing serious crimes, such as murder.

- Terrorists and murderers deserve to die. If you commit a terrible crime you deserve an equally terrible punishment.

- The death penalty protects the public, as it stops the offender being able to commit another serious crime.

- The average term served by prisoners given life imprisonment is about 15 years. What guarantee is there that they will not commit a serious crime on their release?

- It is much cheaper to execute someone, as the cost of life imprisonment is enormous – at present-day prices it would cost around £375 000 to keep a person in prison for 15 years.

? Questions

1 What is meant by the Home Detention Curfew scheme?

2 What are the advantages and disadvantages in using electronic tagging as a form of punishment?

3 Why do some people see community service orders as a 'soft' option?

4 What are the advantages of this type of punishment for the offender and the community?

For discussion

Organize a class debate on 'The death penalty has no place in a civilized society' or 'The death penalty should be reintroduced for murder and terrorism'. WO2.1

For research

The human rights organization Amnesty International opposes capital punishment. Find out the reasons why by visiting its website. IT2.1

Christianity

> **Aim**
> To understand the Christian teaching concerning:
> - crime and the law
> - responses to crime and the aims of punishment.

Christians believe that sin and wrongdoing began with the 'Fall'. This was the Original Sin, which took place in the Garden of Eden (Genesis 3). Some take the story as literally what happened and others believe that it is symbolic of how wrongdoing has caused problems in the world. After human nature became flawed no generation has escaped its effects.

The law

In some countries there is a direct link between the church and the state, for example, in Britain bishops in the House of Lords have played their part in the law making process. In principle, Christianity teaches that it is right to obey the government and uphold the laws of the country. God brought the world into existence not for chaos but for order. In Romans 13: 1–5, Paul explains that God has put the authorities in charge to protect the good from those who do evil. In verse 9 Paul repeats the golden rule of Christianity, *'Love your neighbour as you love yourself.'*

Sometimes there are situations where the law of the country and the command to love one's neighbour have been in conflict. In these circumstances, many Christians have campaigned for a change in the law, for example, in South Africa, many Christians, like Archbishop Desmond Tutu, worked to overcome the laws of apartheid (policies and laws segregating racial groups), as they regarded them as unjust and wrong. In the USA, a Baptist minister, Dr Martin Luther King, led the campaign for civil rights for the non-whites. Usually, the protest takes the form of peaceful demonstrations or actions, but some Christians in South America have supported violent action against the authorities in their struggle for the poor and oppressed. If a law is seen as contrary to the will of God, then Christians believe it right to oppose it.

Forgiveness

Christians believe that Jesus was totally innocent of all wrongdoing and yet he was put to death by crucifixion. What could be more unjust, evil or cruel? Even so, Jesus asked God to forgive those who had committed such a terrible crime against him. As a result, Christians believe that the love and grace of God has made forgiveness possible. There are two relevant principles that evil should be conquered by good (Romans 12: 19–21) and justice should be tempered with mercy (Matthew 18: 23–35).

Within Christianity there is a strong belief that wrongdoers should be forgiven if they repent. Jesus' teaching in the Parable of the Unmerciful Servant (Matthew 18: 21–35) and the reply that Jesus gave to Peter illustrates this.

> *'Then Peter came to Jesus and asked, "Lord, if my brother keeps on sinning against me, how many times do I have to forgive him? Seven times?" "No, not seven times," answered Jesus, "but seventy times seven."'*
>
> (Matthew 18: 21–2)

Jesus taught his followers to ask God to *'Forgive us the wrongs we have done, as we forgive the wrongs that others have done to us'.*

In the Roman Catholic tradition, when something wrong has been done, the person concerned is encouraged to confess to a priest. Penance can then be performed to make up for the wrong action.

Punishment

Most Christians believe that punishment and forgiveness can go together, but there should be a strong emphasis on reform. The aim should be to bring reconciliation between the criminal and society. This is not seen as being 'soft' on crime, but trying to design the punishment so that it helps to rehabilitate the offender and change his or her behaviour.

Prison

Prison sentences may be necessary to protect society, deprive offenders of their freedom and prevent criminals from continuing with their wrongdoing.

Prisoners should not, however, be deprived of reasonable living conditions, nor should prison be a place of physical torture. Retribution (revenge) should not be the reason for imprisoning criminals. Many Christians have been involved in campaigning for prison reform. Elizabeth Fry (1780–1845), a member of The Society of Friends (Quakers), regularly visited Newgate Prison to try to help the women and children who were forced to live in terrible conditions. She campaigned against capital punishment and for the reform of conditions in prisons.

Many denominations appoint prison visitors or prison chaplains who visit offenders and try to help them overcome their problems.

Alternatives to prison

Many Christians support alternative methods of dealing with crime. For example, The Society of Friends (Quakers) are deeply concerned that prison can badly damage people and that with the exception of dangerous criminals, other forms of sentencing are preferable. The completion of community service orders, or the making of reparation to their victims, are regarded as possible alternatives. These punishments avoid the offender's families being punished and are seen as more likely to encourage the law breaker not to re-offend.

Capital punishment

Christians have different views on whether capital punishment should be law. Many believe it is a clear biblical principle – 'a life for a life' – as taught in Genesis 9: 6, Exodus 21: 12 and Leviticus 24: 17. Some support capital punishment on the grounds that it acts as a deterrent and prevents more murders. Many are not convinced that the evidence supports this view.

> 'There is substantial doubt that capital punishment has any significant deterrent effect.'
>
> (Report on Proceedings, 1983 Anglican Synod)

Many Christians oppose the death penalty because there is a real concern that innocent people might be executed and that the possibility of repentance is permanently lost.

Pope John Paul II issued an encyclical in March 1995 that stated that execution is only appropriate 'in cases of absolute necessity, in other words, when it would not be possible otherwise to defend society'.

Lord Longford began visiting prisoners in the 1930s. His visits included those to Myra Hindley and Dennis Neilson

? Questions

1 Give an example of a biblical teaching that encourages obeying the law.

2 Describe Christian teaching concerning forgiving those who have done wrong.

3 What do many Christians believe should be the main aim of punishment?

4 Describe Christian attitudes towards prison, community service orders and capital punishment.

💬 For discussion

1 If the offender is not a dangerous criminal why might many Christians look for an alternative to locking a person up in prison?

2 'Christians are soft on crime.' How far do you agree? Give reasons for your opinion.

> ## Aim
> To understand the Muslim teaching concerning:
> - crime and the law
> - responses to crime and the aims of punishment.

The law

To Muslims, the Qur'an and the Sunnah (practice of the prophet Muhammad) are the basis for all laws. Muslims believe that they must submit to the will of Allah and follow the Shari'ah (Islamic law). Few Muslim countries follows Islamic law as its entire legal system, though Saudi Arabia follows the criminal law of Shari'ah. As Allah sees everything, giving in to temptation and committing a crime or sinning is a foolish thing to do. The most serious or first order sin is known as **shirk** and a person practising it is a **mushrik**. This is the sin of holding something or someone up as being as important as Allah. The second order sins are actions like murder, suicide, sex outside of marriage and theft. The third order sins include cursing and lying.

Forgiveness

Muslims do not see punishment as a way to atone for sin, as only Allah can forgive.

In considering a crime against society, repentance does not mean that the person committing it should go unpunished. The principle is one of honour tempered with mercy. To ignore the fact that a crime has been committed would be wrong and the demands for justice from the wronged person have to be satisfied before the wrongdoer can be forgiven. It is considered better in Islam to forgive, providing the refusal to take revenge is consistent with honour. In the Hadith, Allah told Muhammad that the prophet must forgive those who wronged him.

Punishment

Muslims believe that they have a duty to deter people from committing crimes and to protect society from wrongdoing. In countries where Islam is the main religion, offenders may be locked up in prisons, but many of the punishments take place in public. To Muslims, it is important that people can witness that justice has taken place. Stealing is regarded as being particularly dishonourable, and the Qur'an says:

> *'As to the thief, male or female, cut off their hands: a punishment by way of an example.'*
>
> (Surah 5: 41)

Where theft has occurred because of desperate need, or if there is any doubt or other extenuating circumstances, then this punishment is not given. If the person is a persistent thief and there appears to be no chance of reforming his or her character, then amputation may take place in order to deter others. The penalty for committing adultery is a public flogging.

Corporal punishment may also be used when someone has made defamatory (insulting) remarks against a person.

Capital punishment

Most Muslim countries have the death penalty. Two crimes attract the death sentence – murder, or if someone openly attacks Islam in such a manner as to threaten it, having previously been a believing Muslim. When a murder had been committed Muhammad accepted the justice of 'a life for a life'. The relatives of the dead person may instead choose to forgive or to accept financial compensation.

> *If a man is slain unjustly, his heir shall be entitled to satisfaction.'*
>
> (Surah 17: 33)

> ## ❓ Questions
> 1 What is the Shari'ah?
> 2 What is the most serious sin?
> 3 Why do Muslims believe that even if a person repents he or she should be punished?
> 4 Describe, using examples, the Muslim attitude towards punishment.

🗣 For discussion

Do you think that it is a good idea to let the victims or their families have a say in what punishment the offender should receive?

Aim

To understand the Jewish teaching concerning:

- crime and the law
- responses to crime and the aims of punishment.

The law

A large amount of the **Torah** is devoted to law and includes 613 **mitzvot** (rules or commandments for living). These laws prohibit certain actions and command others, and all but three may be broken if the purpose is to save life. The exceptions are murder, worshipping idols and adultery. Many of the rules are concerned with keeping the Jewish faith, for example, the food laws, such as eating pork or ham, or mixing milk and meat dishes.

Jews believe that it is important that there is the rule of law and order and that there is justice for all.

The Jewish court, the **Bet Din**, consists of three rabbis who make judgement in religious matters and other issues of disagreement between Jews. They do not replace the state law courts.

Repentance, atonement and mercy

Jews believe that if they repent of their wrongdoing and try to make amends for what they have done wrong (atonement), then God is merciful and will forgive.

> '*When God was about to create the world, He thought, "If I create it with mercy alone then sinners will multiply; if I create it with justice alone how will the world endure? I shall therefore create it with both justice and mercy, and in this way it might endure."*'

(Midrash)

Jews believe that God accepts the prayer of a person who is genuine in repentance and gives to charity and fasts. On the Day of Atonement amends are made for the past year's behaviour. Confession, prayer and repentance take place in the synagogue, nothing is eaten or drunk for 25 hours and money is promised to charity.

Punishment

Prevention and rehabilitation are at the centre of the Jewish approach to criminal justice. The aim is not retribution and vengeance, as Ezekiel 33: 11 says, '*I, the Sovereign Lord … do not enjoy seeing sinners die. I would rather see them stop sinning and live.*'

The teaching of '*eye for eye*' (Exodus 21: 24) is not taken in Judaism as an excuse for revenge. In the Talmud it is referred to as paying money to make up for the wrong that has been done.

The prison system is supported, as it is recognized that society needs to be protected. Rabbis and rabbinical students visit and counsel prisoners and help prisoner's families.

Capital punishment

The Torah lists several offences that may be punished by capital punishment, but it is very rarely carried out. Murder may be punishable by capital punishment, but two independent witnesses would be required to have seen the killing. Circumstantial evidence would not be enough to sentence a person to death. The death penalty exists primarily as a deterrent. Judaism sees it as important that the murderer has the opportunity to atone for the wrong he or she has done.

? Questions

1 What is a Bet Din and what is its function?
2 Explain what Jews believe about repentance, atonement and mercy.
3 Describe the main aims of punishment in Judaism.
4 What do Jews believe about capital punishment.

For discussion

Discuss the fairness of the Jewish idea of 'eye for eye, foot for foot …'.

For research

Find out more about the way Jews treat offenders at the Aleph Institute on the Internet. Record your findings.

Buddhism

> ### Aim
> To investigate the Buddhist teaching concerning:
> - crime and the law
> - responses to crime and the aims of punishment.

The concept of sin in the sense of turning away from God does not exist in Buddhism. The primary concern of Buddhism is not with sin, but with suffering. Buddhists believe that the roots of all evil is greed (lobha), hatred (dosa) and ignorance (avijja). The main problem lies in unawareness, false views and lack of wisdom that clouds the mind.

The law

Upholding the law is the ideal as far as Buddhists are concerned. The idea of karma, that 'you reap what you sow', is central to a Buddhist's view of crime and punishment. Every good motive bears good fruit and contributes towards enlightenment. On the other hand, bad actions result in bad karma that might mean rebirth in a lower form. Many Buddhists believe that the only effective punishment is that which we inflict upon ourselves – sooner or later.

Punishment

The importance of protecting people from criminals is recognized by Buddhists. It is seen as necessary to have a system of rewards and punishments for good and bad actions. In Buddhism there is an emphasis on the need to protect criminals from creating more bad karma for themselves. A punishment that deliberately destroys another being implies that there is no other way that the person can learn from his or her mistakes. There is no support for punishments, such as cutting off the hand that steals or stoning a woman who has committed adultery. The ideal is to get criminals to see the error of their ways and to reform (change their behaviour). It is the heart and mind that needs to be changed.

Capital punishment

Some Buddhists are not opposed to the threat of the death penalty providing, as far as possible, it is not carried out. Some suggest banishment or imprisonment as an alternative, while others believe that nothing can excuse the taking of life. Most do not believe in retribution as it goes against the Buddhist teaching of loving kindness (metta) and compassion (**karuna**).

> '"Taking life" means to kill anything that lives. The precept says that you should not strike or kill any living being.
>
> "Anything that lives" is anything that has what is called the "life-force". This includes all members of the animal kingdom as well as humans.
>
> "Taking life" means killing or trying to kill deliberately, by word or action … When it comes to human beings, the killing is considered to be worse if the person killed was a good (virtuous) person.
>
> Apart from that, the seriousness of the offence is also measured by how much the murderer wanted the killing to happen.'
>
> (Buddhaghosa)

> ### ? Questions
> 1 Briefly explain what Buddhists believe about the root causes of evil.
> 2 Explain why Buddhists believe that keeping the law is the right thing to do.
> 3 What forms of punishment do Buddhists not favour?
> 4 What should be the main aim of punishment to a Buddhist?
> 5 Explain the Buddhist attitudes towards capital punishment.

For discussion

'A bad person is someone who hasn't discovered their potential for good.' How far do your agree? Give reasons for your opinion.

Aim

To investigate the Hindu teaching concerning:

*   crime and the law
*   responses to crime and the aims of punishment.

In Hinduism it is often impossible to tell the difference between sin and crime. The Sanskrit term **paapa** is used for either. Hindus believe that bad karma results from a wrong action. To avoid this, penance is required.

The law

Hindus are expected to avoid anti-social behaviour (paapa). The purpose of the law is to protect people and to enable them to carry out their **dharma** (duty).

Punishment

In Hindu scriptures the severity of the suggested punishment depended on the position or status (the **Varna**) of the criminal in society. The lower the caste, the more severe was the punishment that was usually decreed. A Brahmin was not allowed to receive corporal punishment or the death sentence – *'in the case of a Brahmin no corporal punishment must be inflicted'* (Vishnusmriti 5: 2). Rules, like those found in Manusmriti 8: 280 and Vishnusmriti 5: 19, suggest that those of a lower caste who insult a superior should be deprived of the limb that caused the offence. The threat of being relegated, both in this and the next life, to a lower caste acted as a powerful deterrent.

In Hindu scriptures it is clear that the king (or the government) has a duty to protect members of society and give suitable punishment (**danda**) to offenders. For example, the performance of penance could be required. Danda has three parts:

*   retribution
*   protection (imprisonment of the criminal)
*   reformation.

Capital punishment

Hindu teaching does not oppose capital punishment, for example, *'great criminals should all be put to death'* (Vishnusmriti 5: 1). Included were robbers, thieves, adulterous wives and men who have intercourse with a woman of a lower caste. The murderer's intention is considered, so not all cases of murder attracted the death penalty, for example, self defense, or protection of others – *'by killing an assassin the slayer incurs no guilt'* (Manusmriti 8: 351). The death penalty for murder and treason exists in India because it is seen as justified.

On the other hand not all Hindus support the ideas of retribution or revenge. For example, during the time of peaceful protest against British rule in India, Mahatma Gandhi said:

'When a person claims to be non-violent, he is expected not to be angry with one who has injured him. He will not wish him harm; he will wish him well; he will not swear at him; he will not cause him any physical hurt. He will put up with all the injury to which he is subjected by the wrongdoer.'

Gandhi was following the Hindu principle of **ahimsa** (non-violence).

? Questions

1   What is meant by paapa?
2   What do Hindus believe results from wrong action?
3   Explain the relation in Hindu scriptures between caste and punishment.
4   Explain what is meant by danda.
5   Explain Hindu attitudes towards capital punishment.

For discussion

'All members of society should expect the same justice, so the same form of punishment should always be given for a particular crime.' How far do you agree? Give reasons for your opinion.

Aim

To investigate the Sikh teaching concerning:

* crime and the law
* responses to crime and the aims of punishment.

Sikhs believe that everyone has the natural tendency to do wrong things. With God's grace and a real effort, humans can look to God for guidance to lead a good life. Without God's help, the evil passions of anger, greed, lust, pride and worldly attachments affect judgement and cause people to do wrong.

The law

Sikhs teach that the law must protect the weaker members of society from criminals. The key principle to good law is justice. Sikhs are to obey the laws of the country in which they live unless these conflict with Sikh principles. For example, in 1975 Sikhs in Britain opposed having to wear crash helmets when riding a motorbike as it would have involved removing their turbans.

Punishment and forgiveness

Many Sikhs believe that, according to the law of karma, individuals are likely to suffer for their wrongdoing, either in this life or in a future birth. Some offences are specifically religious although they may not break the law of the country. If a Sikh started smoking or cut his or her hair, this would be a religious offence as it contravenes the **Reht Maryada** (code of discipline). Offenders are required to apologize publicly to the congregation and perform whatever penance is recommended. The punishment may include such things as repeating the hymn Japji a set number of times, or service in the gurdwara, such as looking after the worshippers' shoes.

Sikh teaching does not encourage retribution and retaliation, but stresses the importance of trying to be like God who is without hatred (**nirvair**).

Sikhs recognize that people need protection from dangerous criminals and so they accept the need to send some criminals to prison. It is hoped that a person's anti-social behaviour will change and that the offenders will be able to return to society and become useful citizens. Sikhs are encouraged to forgive, as shown in the following example:

> *'Farid, if someone hits you*
> *Do not hit him back.*
> *Go home – after kissing his feet.'*

(Adi Granth: 1378)

Capital punishment

Most Sikhs oppose capital punishment on the grounds that executing a prisoner is without excuse, and would be 'killing in cold blood'. People did not receive the death penalty during the time of Ranjit Singh (1780–1839). This is the only time Sikhs have formed an independent nation. On the one occasion when Sikhs were able to make laws of their own, capital punishment was not used. On the other hand, some Sikhs are not totally opposed to the death penalty. They believe that the threat of capital punishment may provide a deterrent to protect the rest of society.

? Questions

1 How do Sikhs explain why people do things that are wrong?
2 Explain the Sikh attitude towards the law.
3 What is meant by the Reht Maryada and what action should be taken if it is broken?
4 Give an example from the Adi Granth, which encourages forgiveness rather than retaliation.
5 Explain the Sikh attitude towards capital punishment.

For discussion

'It is far more important to keep the law of the land than any religious code.' How far do you agree? Give reasons for your opinion.

Aim

To review a summary of the important issues concerning religious attitudes to crime and punishment and to study some exam questions.

Now that you have considered the difficult religious issues on crime and punishment, it is time to see if you can answer the type of question that will appear in exams. Before you do so, have a look at the factfile summary to check how much you know.

Factfile summary

I need to make sure that I:

- understand the beliefs and teachings in my chosen religion(s) concerning human nature, wrongdoing and the punishment of offenders and repentance and forgiveness.

- understand the different types of crime, for example, those against the person, property, the state, and religious offences.

- understand the causes of crime.

- am aware of the aims of punishment (protection, retribution, deterrence, reformation and vindication) and am able to compare these with the teachings of the religion(s) I have studied.

- understand the effectiveness of different forms of punishment, the cost to society and alternatives to imprisonment, for example, community service orders.

- know about issues such as the handling of young offenders, early release and parole and the debate about capital punishment.

Exam questions

a   Explain why religious people might sometimes consider it right to break the law. [5 marks]

b   Explain religious attitudes towards criminals. [10 marks]

c   'Execution is less degrading and inhuman than keeping someone locked up in prison for life.' How far do you agree? Give reasons for your answer, showing that you have thought about more than one point of view. Refer to religious teachings in your answer. [5 marks]

2   a   Explain the main aims of punishment. [5 marks]

b   Capital punishment (the death penalty) is still used in many countries. Explain how the beliefs and teachings of the religion(s) might affect the attitudes of believers towards capital punishment. [10 marks]

c   'Religious people should always obey the laws of their country.' How far do you agree with this view? Give reasons for your opinion and include different points of view. Refer to the religion(s) you have studied. [5 marks]

3   a   Explain the main causes of crime. [5 marks]

b   Explain religious attitudes towards imprisonment and other forms of punishment. [10 marks]

c   'Young offenders should be given a real shock and be punished severely. That'll teach them not to break the law.' How far do you agree with this view? Give reasons for your opinion and include different points of view. Refer to the religion(s) you have studied. [5 marks]

The rich

Aim
To investigate wealth in Britain, including some of the reasons that help to make some people rich. Citizenship 1e

Who are the rich?

There are more rich people in Britain than ever before. Many employees receive high wages or salaries, many businesses have been extremely successful, the value of property has risen, and hundreds have become millionaires because of the National Lottery. There are thousands of very well-off people living in Britain, and in the south east of England in particular. Their money is often seen in their lifestyle. Expensive cars, luxury homes, designer clothing, gifts, parties and holidays are all part of the scene. They are the envy of those who would love to have their income.

'Filthy rich'

27 out of the top 50 richest people in the world are Americans, including six of the top 10. Many of these have made their fortune in new technologies, such as computers, telecommunications, the Internet and software. For example, in 2000 Bill Gates of Microsoft was reported to have had a personal fortune of £53 billion. Some new businesses have had huge success and people have become multimillionaires in a very short time when these companies have been floated on the stock market. Sometimes the bubble does burst and bankruptcies may result, but many business people are among the richest members of society.

The United Nations Development Report said that in 1996, the 358 wealthiest people in the world have wealth equal to the combined income of 2.3 billion people – well over 40 per cent of the world's population. In 1997, it was reported that the richest 20 per cent of the world's population had 74 times the income of the poorest 20 per cent. Just three people in the world had assets greater than the combined gross national product (GNP) of the least developed countries with their 600 million people.

A survey conducted by *The Sunday Times* in 2000, stated that the top 1000 wealthiest people in Britain were worth a total of nearly £146 billion. That was almost £31 billion more than the previous year. Heading the British rich list was Hans Rausing, the British-based Swedish industrialist. His fortune was reported as being worth £4 billion. Not included in the list was the Queen. If she had been, she would have headed the British list.

Many have made a fortune on the stock market, but shares can also fall very dramatically, as in the Wall Street Crash of 1929 in the USA.

In 1999 the British top earner averaged £70 000 an hour. Bernie Ecclestone averaged more per hour than most people earn in a couple of years. Altogether he netted £617 million by selling a 50 per cent stake in Formula One racing. This compared with David and Victoria Beckham earning around £7 million. Harry Potter author J. K. Rowling was the highest earning woman with £25 million.

Bernie Ecclestone earns more money than most people could ever dream of

In 2001, the Abbey National bank reported that it believes there are around 4 million people in Britain who have at least £50 000 to invest. These figures excluded the value of houses. Is it fair that some are so rich while others are so poor?

Inheritance

Some people inherit wealth. When a relative or friend dies, as heir to their estate they receive their property. Many people have suddenly become very wealthy in this way. According to *The Sunday Times* survey in 2000, 258 out of the top 1000 of Britain's richest people inherited their fortune. The cost of land and property, particularly in the south east of England, means that many more people will become rich as a result of inheritance.

Inheritance tax is payable on very large amounts. The inheritance tax threshold stood at £244 000 in 2001. No tax is payable up to the threshold. The value of property over this amount is taxed at a current rate of 40 per cent.

'Fat cats'

'Fat cats' is a term given to the top company executives who are receiving enormous annual salaries and bonuses from their companies.

A survey of 77 UK companies for *The Guardian* in 1999 revealed that the average annual pay of the top executives was nearly £1 million. On top of this, many received windfalls from share options, which in 10 cases were more than £1 million. 14 of the top 30 executives work for three companies – Cadbury Schweppes, EMI and Amvescap. The top earner for 1998 was Jan Leschy, the chief executive of the drugs company SmithKline Beecham. It is claimed that he received a staggering £92 million from his salary, shares and various perks.

The UK 'fat cats' earn more than elsewhere in Europe because there is a greater use of profit-related pay and shares than in other European countries. With performance-related pay, management receives very large bonuses when the company is successful. Is it right to pay such a large salary to anyone?

? Questions

1 Which new technologies in particular have helped people to become rich?
2 Give some examples of the really wealthy in Britain and state how they have obtained their fortunes.
3 What is meant by inherited wealth?
4 On what is inheritance tax paid?
5 What does the term 'fat cats' mean?
6 Why do UK 'fat cats' earn more than those in other parts of Europe?

🗨 For discussion

1 Some people say that society can be divided into the exploiters and the exploited. What do you think this means? Do you think it is true? Give reasons. C2.1a

2 Is it morally right that the rich are getting richer and the poor are getting poorer? Give reasons. C2.1a; Citizenship 3a

◆ For research

Look in the newspapers and magazines for some examples of the very rich and the very poor. Organize a small group discussion about their financial circumstances. C2.1a; WO 2.1

The poor

Aim
To investigate the problem of poverty in Britain. Citizenship 1a

Poverty

The Universal Declaration of Human Rights declares that:

'all human beings are born free and equal in dignity and rights ...freedom from fear and want has been proclaimed as the highest aspiration of the common people ... to promote social progress and better standards of life in larger freedom.'

Yet millions are barely able to make ends meet. They struggle to survive and provide the basic necessities for life – food, shelter and clothing. The concise Oxford Dictionary defines poverty as *'not having the minimum income level to get the necessities of life'*. This is absolute poverty and applies to millions in the developing countries. Well over one billion people have no access to clean water or an adequate house.

In Britain, very few people live in conditions like this. Does this mean that we have no poverty? Families in Britain that cannot afford to have electricity, a cooker, a telephone and a television are considered to be in poverty. This is poverty when compared to most families. This is relative poverty.

Relative poverty is measured against the average standard of living of a community or country. If the disadvantaged in Britain were living in the poorest countries, they would be among the richest members of the community. In terms of living in Britain, they are poor.

Britain's poor

According to the Department of Social Security's annual survey of households, the number of people living in poverty in Britain is at the highest level ever.

- Households receiving less than the average income grew from 14.1 million in 1996–7 to 14.3 million in 1998–9. This means that three million children are living below the poverty line in families with incomes of less than 60 per cent of the average income.

- A good education helps people break out of poverty. Statistics show that children of poor families are far less likely to do well in school compared with those whose parents are well off.

- The Consumers' Association reported in 1999 that over one million people are so poor in Britain that they cannot pay for either gas or electricity supplies.

- The charity, Help the Aged, says that among the elderly, one in three spend 20 per cent of their income on trying to keep warm. Up to 50 000 people die each year in Britain because they cannot afford enough heating.

Three quarters of a billion people do not have adequate protein or energy from their food supplies and have no access to modern health services

How the government helps the poor

The Beveridge Report of 1942 became the foundation for the modern welfare state. The report argued that it needed the government to tackle the major social problems, such as unemployment, poverty and ill health. The 1945 Act that followed included social insurance to provide for old age, unemployment and sickness. Family allowance provided some support for families with children.

Other methods of help have been introduced, such as income support. This is a means-tested benefit payable to people who are not in full-time employment. The amount paid depends on the family size and type. It represents the minimum income that the Government thinks is enough for the family to live on. Other support includes:

- pensions for the elderly
- job-seekers allowance
- housing benefit
- disability living allowance
- sickness, invalid and incapacity benefit
- free school meals
- child benefit.

Minimum wage

To stop employees being paid very low wages, there is a national minimum wage. This minimum wage is increased every year, but there was outrage when the government announced in February 2000, that the standard minimum wage would rise by 10 pence to £3.70 an hour, as from October 2000.

Many employees thought that a 10 pence rise was an insult

The rate has now risen to over £4 per hour, but not everyone benefits from the National Minimum Wage Act. This includes workers under 18, apprentices, the self-employed, au pairs and nannies. The minimum wage is less for the 18–21-year-olds.

The National Minimum Wage Act covers the following groups of people:

- Full-time, part-time and casual workers
- Home and freelance workers
- Temporary and agency workers
- Pensioners (if they are working)
- Piece workers (people who are paid by the job that is done and not the time that it takes).

Many businesses opposed the minimum wage, as they feared it would costs jobs. The Government believed that it was important to protect people from being under paid. Approximately one in twelve benefit from it, which is around 1.9 million workers. Does the minimum wage have any impact on poverty in Britain? The answer is only a limited one. One third of those benefiting are not the head of households. They are young people living at home, or married women living with employed husbands.

? Questions

1 What does the Universal Declaration of Human Rights say about poverty?
2 What is the difference between absolute and relative poverty?
3 Give examples of how the government attempts to help the poor.

For discussion

1 Do you think that having a national minimum wage will make much difference in the fight against poverty? Citizenship 1h
2 Set up a role-play situation to discuss the problems of poverty. C2.1a; WO2.1

For research

Check out the social security benefit and standard of living statistics in Britain on the Internet. Make a table of the key results and discuss the trends that the figures show. C2.1a; IT2.1

Unemployment and homelessness

Aim
To investigate the problems of unemployment and homelessness.

Unemployment

When people are unemployed there is no wage packet or salary coming into a home each week and many families have to live on a limited income.

Unemployment figures rise and fall as a result of several factors, including the state of the economy. If there is a healthy growing economy, with low interest rates, employers are encouraged to expand their businesses and take on extra workers. If there is overproduction in a particular area, or if the economy slows down, employees may lose their jobs. Employers cut their workforce because labour costs are expensive. More automation can mean fewer people are required. Jobs are then hard to get. Without support from the government, families would be without any income at all. Some of the taxes collected from those in work are used to give an income to those who are unemployed.

Causes of unemployment

One extreme view of some people is that because the government gives the unemployed income support, they are not given the incentive to find jobs. They suggest that some unemployed people are simply lazy and live off the state. Without the support of the welfare state, they say, lazy people would be forced to look for work or go hungry. Others point out that this is not the case. There are many reasons why people may be unemployed. Employment can be difficult to find without educational qualifications or the necessary skills. Getting work may be difficult for those who lose their jobs at the age of 50 and over. For a variety of reasons, some people may not be employable.

In recent years employment patterns have changed and fewer people expect to have one job for life as used to be the case. There has been an increase in part-time, insecure and low paid employment. This has contributed to the poverty in Britain.

Twenty-first century Britain still has thousands who sleep rough on the streets

Homelessness

In 1999, 166 760 people were accepted as homeless by local authorities in England. That could be as many as 400 000 people. There are thousands in bed and breakfast accommodation, living on the streets, or surviving in hostels or squats. Twenty-first century Britain still has a housing problem. Around 78 000 couples or lone parents share accommodation because they cannot afford to set up a home of their own. It is said that nearly half a million households live in overcrowded homes. Nearly three million households live in poor housing conditions.

Reasons for homelessness

There are many reasons why people are homeless. There is a real shortage of affordable homes in this country. House prices are high and well out of the reach of millions. Average house prices rose between 1995 and 1999 from £61 000 to £92 000. That is an increase of 50 per cent in five years.

During 1999, 30 000 owners lost their homes because they could not afford to pay the mortgage.

Even the cost of renting local authority housing is not cheap. In the 10 years from 1988/89 to 1998/99, the average weekly rent for council tenants more than doubled from £19.00 to £42.80. For housing association tenants rents increased during the same period from an average of £24.97 to £53.80. People without a steady income struggle to afford a home.

Helping the homeless

Local authorities have to find bed and breakfast accommodation for those who are homeless within their area. The cost is enormous (over £118 million in 1998/9), but still some people live on the streets. The government aims to reduce those sleeping rough in the major cities. Work done by voluntary agencies, such as Crisis, Shelter, Providence Row and the Salvation Army, help to provide people with hostels rather than letting them sleep in cardboard boxes on the street.

Local authorities have waiting lists of those who want a home. When a person registers, his or her need is assessed according to a variety of factors. Points are awarded and when local authority accommodation becomes available those with the most points are offered the property. Single people do not fair well under this system and are usually at the bottom of the list. As a result, many do not even bother to register. They are forced to look for somewhere that becomes available in the private sector. Such a place is not always easy to find.

? Questions

1. Explain some of the reasons that contribute to people being unemployed.
2. How does the state support the unemployed?
3. Why is it hard for some people to find a job?
4. Why are so many people homeless in Britain?
5. What is being done to help the homeless?

For discussion

1. What right has an unemployed person to expect help from the state? Give reasons. To help with your discussion check the unemployment benefit rates on the Internet. C2.1a; IT2.1

2. Organize a discussion about the problem of homelessness and what should be done to help. Members of the class could play the parts of representatives from the government, the local authority, charities, families who have relatives who are homeless and a homeless family. C2.1a; Citizenship 1f, 2c; WO2.1

For research

In small groups, find out about one of the charities that try to help the homeless. Give a short presentation explaining its work. Useful websites include Shelter and Crisis. Citizenship 1f; IT2.1

Caring for the poor

> ### Aim
> To investigate who should care for the poor, the role of charities and the National Lottery.

Caring for the poor

Who should have the responsibility for caring for the poor in Britain? Is it the responsibility of the individuals themselves to find a way out of their poverty? Do they have a right to expect help? Perhaps they need to work or study and get a better education, or improve their skills. There are thousands who are poor through no fault of their own and are powerless to break out of the poverty trap.

Should it be the responsibility of the rest of the family and relations? Many families are very supportive of each other, but poverty tends to run in families so in many cases this isn't an answer.

Should communities help? Councils, charities and religious organizations give a great deal of help to those in need in their local areas. Sometimes the problems of poverty are widespread in a community. Thousands may be affected by the closing of a major place of work, for example, a large factory, or a whole community could be hit by a major catastrophe, such as the foot and mouth outbreak in farming that particularly hit Cumbria and Devon in 2001. Help is needed on a large scale. This is where the government has a role to play. With major problems like inner city poverty, child poverty or rural poverty, national strategies are required.

Over 140 organizations, including the charity Oxfam, have joined the UK Coalition Against Poverty. The aim is to campaign for a national anti-poverty strategy. People living in poverty are being invited to join in the discussions with MPs, charities and other interested bodies. Working together, it is hoped that progress will be made towards lifting people out of poverty.

Charities

Britain has more voluntary organizations at work in the communities helping those in need than ever before. There are around 200 000 registered charities and 200 000 non-charitable voluntary organizations in the UK. Every year 7000 new charities are registered. Each year half the population takes part in some voluntary work. They give more than 4 billion hours of their time. They do so because they believe that their volunteering provides something that the state is unable to do.

Fears were expressed that with the launch of the National Lottery in 1994, charities would suffer. Donations were down during the first years of the Lottery, but some charity events have grown and grown. In 2000, the BBC Children in Need appeal raised over £12 million in one night. The 2001 Comic Relief Red Nose Day has resulted in over £42 million being donated to help relieve poverty.

National Lottery

The National Lottery was set up for two reasons – to give people the opportunity to win cash prizes of varying sizes and to support good causes. The first National lottery draw took place in November 1994. In 1997 it was extended to include a mid-week draw. Each week people who hope to get rich gamble millions of pounds on the lottery. Gambling is something the human race has been doing for thousands of years. People are thrilled at the prospect of risk. They are attracted to the possibility, however remote, that their lives will be transformed suddenly in a game of chance. Many gamble much more than they can afford.

Not all winners are satisfied with their winnings. Lee Ryan who won millions on the lottery ended up with an 18-month prison sentence because he handled stolen vehicles.

A tragic case involved regular National Lottery player, Tim O'Brien. He bought a ticket with the same numbers each week, but one week he forgot, and that was the week all his numbers came up and he would have won the jackpot. The disappointment was so great that he committed suicide by shooting himself.

Smaller lotteries have been around for many years, as shown by the following song from *The Lottery*, a farce by Henry Fielding (1707–54), that was first perfomed in 1732 in London.

A lottery is a taxation,
Upon all the fools of Creation;
And Heav'n be prais'd,
It is easily rais'd,
Credulity's always in fashion;
For, folly's a fund,
Will never lose ground,
While fools are so rife in the Nation.

(A song from *The Lottery*, a farce by Henry Fielding (1707–54), first performed in 1732)

Well over a thousand National Lottery winners have become millionaires. By February 2001, the lottery had paid over £9.5 billion to good causes. Money has been given under one of five headings:

- the arts
- sport
- national heritage
- projects to mark the millennium
- charities.

Grants include nearly £1.5 billion to the Arts Council of England (around 13 000 projects), more than £1.5 billion to the Heritage Lottery Fund (nearly 7000 projects), nearly £2 billion to the Millennium Commission (over 2000 projects) and nearly £1.5 billion to Sport England (nearly 10 000) projects.

❓ Questions

1 Do you think that it is a good idea to involve lots of groups of people in planning a national strategy to help the poor? Give reasons.

2 Why do you think that the Comic Relief and Children in Need charities have caught the public's imagination? Give reasons.

3 Explain what Henry Fielding was trying to say in the song from *The Lottery*.

4 Which groups have the National Lottery helped?

💬 For discussion

Organize a debate to discuss the good and bad points about a national lottery.
C2.1a; Citizenship 2b; WO2.1

◆ For research

1 Find out some examples of groups that have been helped by the National Lottery.

2 Do you think that the lottery has helped the poor in Britain? Give reasons. IT2.1a

3 Make notes on some of the ways that some charities help the poor. Using the charity's website will usually give information, for example, try the BBC and Comic Relief websites. Citizenship 1f; IT.2.1a

Christianity

> **Aim**
> To investigate Christian views on wealth and helping the poor.

Earning an income

God worked when he created the universe. God gave Adam and Eve the task of looking after the world. After the original sin (the Fall), God told Adam that humans would have to get their food *'by the sweat of their brow'* (see Genesis 3:19). Matthew 25 shows that Christians need to be working, using their talents for God and in helping people and society. Paul taught that it was wrong for people to be lazy and hope that others would look after them.

> *'Whoever refuses to work is not allowed to eat.'*
>
> (2 Thessalonians 3: 9)

This tough attitude is not taken against people who are unemployed through no fault of their own. It applies to those who wish to take advantage of the generosity of Christians, while they make no useful contribution to society themselves.

Wealth

Christians believe that all wealth is God given and that people are responsible as stewards to Him for how they use it.

> *'Remember that it is the Lord your God who gives you the power to become rich.'*
>
> (Deuteronomy 8: 18)

There are some Christians who believe that it is God's wish that they become rich. They believe in prosperity and see nothing at all wrong in becoming millionaires. They argue that as long as they give God a tenth (a tithe) of their income, then the more they earn the better, as so much good can be done with the money.

Most believe that it is more important to love God and not worry too much about material things.

Others prefer not to have too many possessions. The problem with wealth is that people can become greedy. Paul said that *'the love of money is*

the root of all evil' (1 Timothy 6: 10). Jesus told a rich young man to sell all he had and give it to the poor, then follow him, he said:

> *'It is much harder for a rich person to enter the Kingdom of God than for a camel to go through the eye of a needle.'*
>
> (Mark 10: 25)

The important things in life are lost by many that wish to gain a fortune. Jesus warned that heavenly riches are more important than earthly ones.

> *'For your heart will always be where your riches are.'*
>
> (Matthew 6: 21)

Jesus was concerned that people are tempted to get money out of its right position. Some people fall in love with money and it becomes an idol.

> *'No one can be a slave of two masters; he will hate one and love the other; he will be loyal to one and despise the other. You cannot serve both God and money.'*
>
> (Matthew 6: 24)

Gambling

Many Christians view gambling as a sin because they believe that it appeals to greed. Gambling is addictive. It may start with a pound on the National Lottery, but can develop into hundreds of pounds being spent on horse races, football pools and so on. Others believe that there is nothing really wrong with just a 'flutter' on the Grand National horse race or the National Lottery, particularly as a part of the money from the lottery goes to good causes.

Poverty

Christians believe that everyone is in need in some way. All people need the love of God and the very rich can still be spiritually poor. Poverty can be more than not having enough money. For example, it can be experienced through lack of loving relationships, loneliness, illness, worry or unhappiness. Jesus saw in Zacchaeus (the wealthy tax collector) the poverty of his life. He needed help as much as the other sinners and outcasts that he visited.

The Salvation Army collects money, which helps towards providing shelters for the homeless, among many things

Christians teach that money can be used wisely, for example, to help the poor and needy and a tithe (a tenth of one's income) or an offering can be given to the Church or charities. Right from the start of Christianity the followers of Jesus sold their surplus property and possessions and gave the money to the poor.

> *'They would sell their property and possessions, and distribute the money among all, according to what each one needed.'*
>
> (Acts 2: 45)

This was in obedience to the teaching of Jesus in the Sermon on the Mount when he told his followers that one of their religious duties was to give to charity. In the Parable of the Good Samaritan (Luke 10: 25–7), Jesus made it clear that it is important to care for those in need. He condemns those who refuse to help. The rich man in the Parable of the Rich Man and Lazarus (Luke 16: 19–31) does not enter heaven because he ignored the beggar at his door. In the Parable of the Sheep and Goats (Matthew 25: 31–46), Jesus warns that every time a person refuses to help the needy, he or she is refusing to help Jesus. The golden rule of Christianity is to love your neighbour as you love yourself.

Many charities such as Christian Aid, Tear Fund, CAFOD and World Vision are organized by Christians. The Salvation Army has 50 centres in Britain, which provide beds for nearly 5000 people every night.

People like Mother Theresa have been inspired by their Christian beliefs to spend their lives helping the poor. Until her death, she worked in India with the Sisters of Charity helping the sick, orphans, homeless and the poor.

? Questions

1 Explain how Christians who are rich might justify their wealth.

2 What did Jesus mean when he said, *'It is much harder for a rich person to enter the Kingdom of God than for a camel to go through the eye of a needle'*?

3 Explain Christian beliefs about the dangers of money?

4 What does it mean to be spiritually poor?

5 Explain Christian attitudes towards the poor.

6 Give examples of how Christians try to help the needy.

For discussion

What did Paul mean when he claimed that the love of money is the root of all evil? Do you think he is right? Give reasons. C2.1a; Citizenship 3a

For research

In a small group, find out more details about the work of Christians in helping the poor. Prepare a visual aid and give a presentation to the rest of the class. C2.1b; Citizenship 1f; IT2.1; WO2.1

Aim
To investigate Muslim views on wealth and helping the poor.

Earning an income

Working to earn an income is very important in Islam. It is the duty of a Muslim man to earn enough money for his own and his family's needs.

'No one eats better food than that which they have earned by their own labours.'

(Hadith)

It is not acceptable to gain wealth by laziness, cheating, stealing and gambling. Interest on money lent is not demanded as this exploits those in need.

Wealth

Allah creates all wealth and it is His property. Muslims believe that they should be grateful for whatever God has given to them. It is wrong to think that you are superior to someone who has less. Being greedy and mean are great evils. Wealth and money is only of value for the good it can do.

All lotteries are gambling and **haraam** (not allowed) to Muslims.

'Believers, wine and games of chance, idols and divining arrows, are abominations devised by Satan. Avoid them, so that you may prosper.'

(Surah 5: 90)

Mukhtar Mohidin, a Muslim factory worker from Blackpool, won millions on a lottery. It wasn't a happy story, as he was criticized by local Muslims for gambling, sued by his wife for half the money and he ended up at the local police station after a family quarrel at a reunion to celebrate his win.

Poverty

As Allah gives wealth he has a right to demand how it should be used. Muslims believe that God expects them to be charitable and to help the poor.

'He who eats and drinks while his brother goes hungry, is not one of us.'

(Hadith)

'He who begs without need is like a person holding a burning coal in his hand.' (Hadith)

Muslims give part of their income as a religious duty (**zakah**). After they have taken care of their family, Muslims give $2\frac{1}{2}$ per cent of the surplus income. There are different rates for goods and crops and so on. In addition, Muslims make voluntary gifts – **sadaqah**. Helping the poor is the compassionate thing to do, but there is a warning against those who try to take advantage of a Muslim's generosity.

Muslims do support those with genuine need and have many charities, including Islamic Relief and The Red Crescent.

? Questions

1 For what purpose is it important for a Muslim to earn an income?

2 In what ways is it not acceptable to obtain money?

3 Explain Muslim teaching concerning gambling and the National Lottery.

4 Explain a Muslim's responsibility towards helping the poor. Include the difference between zakah and sadaqah payments.

For discussion

'There are too many scroungers in society who would take advantage of those who are generous.' Do you agree? Give reasons. C2.1a

Aim
To investigate Jewish views on wealth and helping the poor.

Earning an income

Judaism sees work as a valuable and important way of earning income. Humans are the servants of God, doing his work on earth. In the Ten Commandments, it says, *'You have six days in which to do your work'* (Exodus 20: 9), and the Sabbath is a day of rest.

The importance of gaining an income from work is shown in both the **Torah** and the **Talmud**. Both agree that the tools of a person's trade are not to be taken for the payment of a debt. There is no room for laziness.

> *'Lazy people should learn a lesson from the way ants live … they store up their food during the summer, getting ready for the winter. How long is the lazy man going to lie in bed? … while he sleeps, poverty will attack him like an armed robber.'*
>
> (Proverbs 6: 6–11)

Wealth

Jews believe that wealth comes from God, but that it is wrong to be too caught up in trying to get rich.

> *'Be wise enough not to wear yourself out trying to get rich.'*
>
> (Proverbs 23: 4)

There is a danger that wealth may make a person forget God.

> *'When your cattle and sheep, your silver and gold, and all your other possessions have increased, make sure that you do not become proud and forget the Lord your God.'*
>
> (Deuteronomy 8: 13–14)

It is very easy to be greedy for more and this can then become the centre of life. The Midrash says, *'He who has a hundred, craves for two hundred.'* This motivates a person to gamble. The first reference to gambling in Judaism is Mishnah Sanhedrin 3.3. Professional gamblers (dice players) are recorded as being invalid as witnesses.

Some synagogues in America obtain some of their income from bingo. It is on days like Hanukkah and Purim that most gambling has taken place in the Jewish community. Jews are aware of the addictiveness of gambling and so many urge caution, even in taking part in the National Lottery. In practice, many see nothing wrong in buying a ticket.

Poverty

It is a duty for Jews to give a tenth of their income to the poor as **tzedaka** (charity). This they believe is owed to the poor and failure to pay it is robbing them. Jews keep collecting boxes in their homes, called pushkes. There are many Jewish charities including Jewish Care, United Jewish Communities, the Norwood Orphanages and Jewish hospices. Jews also provide soup kitchens to help feed the hungry and homeless.

Judaism teaches that the best way of helping the poor is to help them to help themselves so that they may become self-supporting.

❓ Questions

1 Why do you think that Jewish teachings forbid the taking of a debtor's tools in payment for a debt?

2 What does the Midrash mean when it says, *'He who has a hundred, craves for two hundred'*?

3 Explain Jewish teachings concerning wealth and riches.

4 What duty do Jews believe they have towards the poor?

5 Give examples of some of the work done by Jews to help the poor, hungry and homeless.

💬 For discussion

Why is it seen as far more important to help people to help themselves than to give them handouts? C2.1a

◆ For research

Make notes about Jews and gambling. Use the Internet to find out more information.

Buddhism

Earning an income

The fifth stage of **The Eightfold Path** is Right Livelihood. Jobs that involve going against the precepts are not allowed, for example, gambling or selling meat, and so on, but Buddhists are not encouraged to be lazy. Buddhists should make a Right Effort and be alert at what they are doing. It is said that the Buddha recommended that each person be *'skilled, efficient, earnest and energetic in whatever profession he is engaged and that he should know it well'* (Rahula 1959: 82). Buddhists monks (particularly in the Theravadin tradition) do not work for money but rely on the generosity of others.

Wealth

Buddhists believe in the Middle Way. This means striking a balance between wealth and poverty. Wealth is seen as only a means to an end, not the goal in life. It creates the conditions under which spiritual progress may flourish.

> *'Wealth is neither good or bad … One can acquire wealth by lawful means without harming others. One can be cheerful and use the wealth without greed or lust. One can be heedful of the dangers of the attachment to wealth and share the wealth with others to perform good deeds. One can be aware that it is not the wealth, nor the good deeds, but liberation from craving and selfish desire that is the goal. In this way, this wealth brings joy and happiness. One holds wealth not for oneself but for all beings.'*
>
> (Anguttara Nikaya)

It is the way wealth is acquired and used that is important. The danger is that we can become physically rich but spiritually poor. The Buddha taught that selfish desires are one of the root causes of suffering and unhappiness. So gambling on the National Lottery in the hope of winning millions is not approved of by Buddhists.

Poverty

Poverty in Buddhism is not a virtue. On the other hand, generosity is one of the most important **lay** Buddhist virtues. Gifts freely given bring great merit and the desire to help the poor is important in Buddhist society. Buddhists do not boast about their charity work and often it goes unnoticed, but in 1987, a Thai monk, Ven Kantayapiwat, was awarded the Norwegian Children's Peace Prize for his work in helping homeless children in rural areas.

Lay Buddhists believe that they have a responsibility to share with the poor. A bhikkhu (monk) is allowed only a minimum of possessions and relies on the Buddhist community to support him.

In Mahayana Buddhism someone who masters the six perfections (generosity, good conduct, patience, energy, meditation and wisdom) is called a bodhisattva.

? Questions

1 What types of jobs are Buddhists not allowed to do?

2 What is the Buddhist attitude towards laziness?

3 Why do some Buddhists not work for money?

4 Explain what the Middle Way means in relation to wealth and poverty.

5 Explain the meaning of the quotation from the Anguttara Nikaya.

6 Why doesn't the National Lottery appeal to most Buddhists?

7 Explain how Buddhists view poverty and caring for the poor.

8 Who is known as a bodhisattva?

For discussion

1 'It is very difficult for anyone who is wealthy not to be materialistic and greedy.' Do you agree? Give reasons. C2.1a

2 'It would be better if the Buddhist monks spent more time actually doing something to help the poor rather than just meditating.' Do you agree? Give reasons. C2.1a; Citizenship 1f, 3a

Aim

To investigate Hindu views on wealth and helping the poor.

Earning an income

Hindus see it as their duty to earn an income. In the past the caste system gave specific jobs to different groups.

- The **Brahmins** were to be priests and provide links with the divine.

- The **Kshatriyas** were to rule, protect and lead society.

- The **Vaishyas** were mainly shopkeepers, traders and farmers.

- The **Shudras** were those who were servants for the other three groups and did the physical work.

Still today, office and professional work is regarded as superior to physical or manual work. All and every work (unless it is against Hindu teaching) is regarded as valuable and no one is encouraged to be lazy.

Krishna is recorded in the Bhagavad Gita as saying, *'Do the work allocated to you according to your dharma, for work is better than idleness'* (Bhagavad Gita 3: 8), and *'A man engaged in the performance of his duties leads his soul towards liberation'* (Bhagavad Gita 18: 45).

Wealth

The goddess Lakshmi is shown as a beautiful woman with four hands. The hands represent the four ends of human life: righteousness, desires, wealth and freedom from the cycle of birth and death.

Gold coins flow from her hands, which suggest that those who worship her gain wealth. Her clothes are red with gold lining, which symbolizes activity and prosperity.

A Hindu may seek wealth and power, but it must be done in a right way. Many Hindus do not think it wrong to gamble or take part in the National Lottery. During the festival of Divali, Hindu businessmen pray to Lakshmi asking for her blessings and generosity. In later life spiritual matters become more important than gaining wealth. It is expected that wealth will be used to help those who are poor.

Poverty

There are many people in Hindu society in modern India who are very poor. Hindus believe that merit can be gained by helping these people. Giving away any surplus is considered a good thing to do, but sacrificial giving is believed to bring unseen merit. Hindus are encouraged to give the gifts in a right manner, as giving just to impress defeats the object. Many Hindu communities expect their members to donate up to 10 per cent of their income. This is for the establishing of facilities for the community, charity work or the building and upkeep of temples.

? Questions

1 How do Hindus view work?

2 When do spiritual matters become more important than obtaining wealth in Hindu tradition?

3 Helping the poor enables Hindus to gain merit. What does this mean?

4 Describe some of the acts of charity expected by the Hindu community.

For discussion

'It is selfish to pray for wealth when so many are poor.' Do you agree? Give reasons. C2.1a

For research

Use the Internet to discover some of the work done by Hindu charities. Record your findings. IT2.1

Sikhism

Earning an income

All Sikhs are instructed to earn honestly and share generously. It does not matter what form the work takes, for example, manual, professional or skilled. Work is seen as essential to provide income for the family. Every able-bodied person has a moral duty to earn a living and do some useful work for society. It is not right when work is available to live off the earnings of others. Begging or not working is lazy and selfish.

> *'He alone has found the right way who eats what he earns through toil and shares his earnings with the needy.'*
>
> (Adi Granth: 1245)

The three duties that a Sikh must carry out can be summed up in three words – pray, work, give.

Wealth

Sikhism points out that there is worry associated with either being rich or being poor.

> *'Those who have money have the anxiety of greed: those without money have the anxiety of poverty.'*
>
> (Adi Granth: 1019)

To be a holy person does not mean that you have to be poor.

> *'Blessed is the godly person and the riches they possess because they can be used for charitable purposes and to give happiness.'*
>
> (Guru Amar Das)

The love of money for its own sake is not encouraged, as one of the five vices is covetousness and greed. Sikhs should not take advantage of the poor in order to get rich and they should avoid gambling. Gambling on the National Lottery in the hope of becoming a millionaire is not the Sikh way. Inheriting wealth is often seen as the karmic reward for good deeds in a previous existence.

Poverty

Sikhs recognize that they have a responsibility towards the poor and those in need. They are reminded that *'God's bounty belongs to all, but in this world it is not shared justly'* (Adi Granth: 1171). Sikhs are therefore encouraged to give all they can to help those living in poverty. Sharing is important and Sikhs give least a tenth (**daswandh**) of their income to others. This does not mean that they give it all in money. Gifts include:

- food donated for the **langar** (free kitchen attached to Sikh temples). For a Sikh, it is a privilege as well as a duty to provide langar (food) in the **gurdwara** for the whole congregation after the service of worship.

- blankets for disaster relief

- building materials for the gurdwara

- giving to charity, for example, for helping the sick or providing shelter for the homeless. Sikhs are involved in charity work, such as building hospitals, care homes, special schools and hospices, and they support many charity organizations, such as Oxfam.

? Questions

1 Why do Sikhs believe that they should work?
2 What is the Sikh attitude towards those who beg and choose not to work?
3 Explain what Sikhs believe about wealth.
4 What is the Sikh view of gambling?
5 Who is responsible for the poor?
6 Describe the practical ways taken by Sikhs to help those in poverty.

💬 For discussion

'For many, the giving a tenth of their income is a real sacrifice.' Do you think that Sikhs are very generous? Give reasons.

Aim

To review a summary of the important issues concerning religious attitudes to the rich and poor in society and to study some exam questions.

Now that you have considered the difficult religious issues concerning the rich and poor in society, it is time to see if you can answer the type of question that will appear in exams. Before you do so, have a look at the factfile summary to check how much you know.

Factfile summary

I need to make sure that I:

- know and understand why poverty and wealth exist.

- know and understand who is responsible for taking care of those who live in poverty.

- know and understand the religious teachings and beliefs concerning the rich and poor.

- know and understand the attitude of religious believers towards wealth and poverty.

- know and understand the work of religious organizations who work to help the poor.

- know about various issues, such as gambling (National Lottery), homelessness and unemployment.

- know and understand the importance of work and earning a living.

- know and understand the main technical terms, for example, minimum wage, 'fat cat' salaries, laziness and inherited wealth.

- am able to evaluate other people's views and express opinions of my own.

Exam questions

1 a Explain the problems that might be faced by someone who suddenly becomes very rich. [5 marks]

b Explain religious attitudes towards wealth and possessions. [10 marks]

c 'It is wrong for a few people to be very rich while many are poor.' How far do you agree? Give reasons for your answer, showing that you have thought about more than one point of view. Refer to religious teachings in your answer. [5 marks]

2 a Explain what the state does to help those suffering from poverty. [5 marks]

b Explain how religious teachings might encourage people to help the poor. [10 marks]

c 'If people are too lazy to work, then they should not be given help.' How far do you agree? Give reasons for your answer, showing that you have thought about more than one point of view. Refer to religious teachings in your answer. [5 marks]

3 a Explain three possible causes of poverty. [5 marks]

b Explain religious attitudes towards the rights of the poor and the responsibilities of the rich in society. [10 marks]

c 'The National Lottery encourages those who can't afford it to gamble and that is immoral.' How far do you agree? Give reasons for your answer, showing that you have thought about more than one point of view. Refer to religious teachings in your answer. [5 marks]

Abstract reasoning forming an argument using ideas

Ahimsa non-violence or non-injury

Allah name for God in Islam

Anglican Communion Christian Churches in fellowship with the Church of England worldwide

Apostles' Creed statement of Christian belief

Artha Hindu idea of wealth

Artefact object used in worship

Ashram Hindu religious community

Bet Din court of Jewish law

Bet Hayyim Jewish cemetery

Blastocyst fertilized ovum at about 5–7 days

Brahmins Hindu caste of priests

The Broadcasting Standards Commission deals with complaints from the public

British Board of Film Classification classifies films

The British National Union of Journalists trade union of journalists

Buddha Siddattha Gotama, the enlightened one, founder of Buddhism, one of the Three Refuges

Calvinists Protestant followers of John Calvin with strong beliefs in justification by faith and predestination

Chalice cup used to hold wine in the mass or communion service

The Child Protection Act, 1978 covers a range of measures to protect children from various forms of abuse

Christ title given to Jesus, means 'anointed one', or Messiah

Conscience way of knowing inside yourself that something is right or wrong

Consumer society society in which people are obsessed with buying things

Corporate worship worship performed together

Covenant agreement between God and His people in Judaism

Crucifix cross with the figure of Jesus on it

Danda punishment in Hinduism

Dasam Granth collection of Sikh sacred writing

Daswandh tenth of income given to charity in Sikhism

Day of Resurrection day when the dead will return to life

Denominations divisions or groups, as in Christian denominations

Dhamma teaching of the Buddha, one of the Three Refuges

Dharma Hindu idea of personal duty or righteousness

The Eightfold Path Follows on from the Four Noble Truths. Divided into three parts:

Wisdom (Right Understanding and Right Intention), Morality (Right Speech and Right Action) and Meditation (Right Effort, Right Mindfulness and Right Concentration).

Embryo fertilized ovum at about 12–14 days when implanted into the wall of the womb

Embryo cloning removal of cell(s) from the embryo to encourage the development of separate embryo(s)

Engaged Buddhism practical application of Buddhism to social activity

Enlightenment total understanding of the nature of existence

Epistles letters

Evangelism spreading the message of the faith

Experience way of 'knowing' the truth because something has happened to you

Experiment scientific method of testing something to see if it is 'true'

The Five Precepts principles of Buddhist morality

Foetus fertilized ovum at about 11 weeks when the organs have developed

The Four Noble Truths these are: 1 Life involves suffering; 2 This is caused by always wanting things; 3 The way to end suffering is to rid yourself of wanting and to find peace in life; 4 This can be worked towards through the Eightfold Path

Giana Sikh able to interpret the Guru Granth Sahib

Granthi Sikh leader of worship in the Gurdwara

Guru teacher

Guru Granth Sahib Holy Book of Sikhism

Gurdwara Sikh place of worship

Gutka collection of Sikh hymns, extracts from the Guru Granth Sahib

Hadith sayings and teaching of Muhammad

Haram anything that is not allowed in Islam

Holy Spirit Christian way of understanding God's power in the world, God

Hypothesis idea used as the starting point for scientific testing

Imam leader of worship in the mosque

Impermanence the idea that everything is in a state of change

The Independent Television Commission controls commercial television companies

Jap a Sikh writing used in daily prayer

Kama Hindu idea of desires

Karma law of cause and effect, belief that what happens in one life affects the next reincarnation, sum of person's actions in life

Karuna the idea of compassion in Buddhism

Ketuvim the third part of the Jewish sacred writings, TeNaKh

Khalsa those people who have taken the initiation ceremony and become members of the ruling body of Sikhism

Kippah Jewish skull-cap

Kshatriyas warrior and ruler caste in Hinduism

Langar communal vegetarian meal shared by Sikhs, place where it is prepared

Lay person who is not ordained as a priest, ordinary members of a faith (the laity)

Mantras sets of recited words in worship, prayer or meditation

Materialism belief in the importance of having possessions in your life

Meditation the practice of deep thought, concentration or study of texts

Mercy killing another term for euthanasia

Messiah means 'anointed one'. In Judaism, it refers to the Kings of Israel and a future leader who will bring in the Messianic Age. In Christianity, it refers to Jesus, the Christ

Messianic Age future time of universal peace when the Messiah has come

Mezuzah a tiny scroll containing part of Jewish scriptures placed in a box and attached to the door posts of homes

Mitzvot rules or commandments (singular – mitzvah)

Moksha release from the cycle of rebirths

Monastic relating to the lifestyle of monks and nuns

Mool Mantra opening lines of the Guru Granth Sahib

Moral absolute ethical statement that is right at all times and in all circumstances

Mukti Sikh idea of release from cycle of death and rebirth

Mushrik Muslim who commits a sin (shirk)

Mysticism various forms of religious practice to become closer to the Divine

Neviim second part of the Jewish sacred writing, the TeNaKh, the books of prophecy

Nirvair being without hatred in Sikhism

Non-conformist Christians who broke away from the Church of England or who formed groups with free forms of worship

Nuclear families families including both parents and their child(ren)

The Obscene Publications Act, 1959 and 1964 provides definition and law on obscenity

Observation gathering evidence by looking

Paapa antisocial behaviour in Hinduism

Pastoral support help received in personal matters

Paten plate used to hold the bread in the mass or communion service

Physical discipline control of the body

Physical movement using movement of the body as part of worship

Piety religious acts such as worship, pilgrimage or charity

The Post Office Act, 1953 controls what can be sent through the post

Prayer words said to God in worship

The Press Complaints Commission deals with complaints against the press

Primitive steak fertilized ovum at about 14 days, when feature that will become backbone appears

Protestant Reformation sixteenth century movement of religious change leading to breaks with the Roman Catholic Church

Puja worship or offerings

Quadi Muslim legal expert

Qur'an Holy Book of Islam

Rabbi Jewish teacher, leader of worship in the synagogue

The Radio Authority licenses and regulates independent radio

Reason use of logical arguments

Rebirth to take on another earthly life

Reht Maryada Sikh code of conduct

Reincarnation to be born again in another form

Relative depending on the time and circumstances

Religious community a group of people from the same religion

Resurrection rising of the dead

Retreat time spent away from normal way of life for religious purposes

Right Action one of the Eightfold Path

Right Intention one of the Eightfold Path

Ritual objects items used in a religious ceremony

Rosary set of beads used to assist prayer or meditation

Sadaqah voluntary gifts

Samsara the cycle of birth, death and rebirth

Sangha the community of all Buddhists, specifically the order of monks, one of the Three Refuges

Self-determination the ability or right to decide what happens to you.

Sewa selfless service to others in Sikhism

Shabbat Jewish day of rest (Sabbath)

Shahadah Muslim statement of belief in one God and the Prophet Muhammad

Shari'ah the Law of Islam

Shirk sin in Islam

Shruti revealed Hindu scriptures

Shudras servants and workers in the Hindu caste system

Siddattha Gotama founder of Buddhism, the Buddha

Skandhas the parts that make up what we would call a human being (forms, feelings, perceptions, thoughts and consciousness)

Smriti remembered Hindu scriptures

Sunnah the example of Muhammad

Symbol an item with a meaning or that represents something

Synagogue Jewish place of worship

Tallit Jewish prayer shawl

Talmud commentary by rabbis on the Torah

Tefillin leather boxes contains passages of scripture attached to forehead and arm

The Telecommunications Act, 1984 controls what can be said or sent by telecommunication

TeNaKh Jewish scriptures, Torah, Neviim and Ketuvim

The Ten Precepts principles of Buddhist morality

Therapeutic cloning removal of DNA from one embryo and its replacement with other DNA

Tipitaka Sutras Buddhist scriptures, the Three Baskets

Torah Jewish book of Law, first part of their scriptures, TeNaKh

Tradition custom, something that has always been done and is therefore true

Tzedakah giving to charity in Judaism

Tzitzit the tassels on the end of Jewish prayer shawls

Ummah brotherhood of all Muslims

Vand Chhakna religious duty to share with others in Sikhism

Varna Hindu idea of position in society, caste

Vaishyas traders and farmers in Hindu caste system

Viable used with reference to life, it is the point at which a foetus could survive if it were to be born

Witness act or speak out on behalf of your faith

Yoga form of physical self-discipline and meditation

Zakah charitable giving as a religious duty to Islam

Zygote newly fertilized ovum